DRAINED

for Gill and Norman
and Sarah

DRAINED

PAUL HART

DEWI LEWIS PUBLISHING

PICTURING THE POLDER

FRANCIS HODGSON

The viewer is just off the tarmac in Paul Hart's view of the tower at the RAF bombing range at Wainfleet, in the Lincolnshire Fens a bit more than five miles from Skegness. It's as though a car has just sounded its horn to demand passage on the narrow lane, just before we get there. There's fog, the road is wet, the little barrier is raised but it isn't a level crossing. That's where the sentries used to stand. The atmosphere is unmistakable: this greyed-out land, far out in the marshes, makes one wary. You can hear the drowsy growl of the aero engines, a barking dog inland. It's a film set, a record cover, a paperback …

Only it isn't. The tower at Wainfleet sleeps 6, has a 360° glazed living room on the top floor with predictably "stunning" views (on a less foggy day you can apparently see Hunstanton, on the other side of The Wash) and a hot tub. It's perfect for a weekend, according to many of the visitors who, between them, have given it 9.4 out of 10 as a place to stay. For Bob from Bristol "this is the best holiday home we have ever rented. The location is a little bleak; it is in a chain link and razor wire compound and has an electric gate. All this serves to add..." The new owners have done the sensible thing, and fixed up the tower to rent. Because here, as elsewhere, there's a new harvest to farm. In the era of globalization one of the crops you can still make money from, where labour costs are so high, is people. They farm people here now. Everything changes.

The flat Fens are maybe the least known corner of England, even to the English. The Fens are alien, mysterious. In some very real part of English psychology, the Fens are foreign. That may partly be why an internal tourist trade is growing there from other parts of England.

You have to imagine that The Wash used to be much bigger, the great square shallow inlet of the North Sea on the eastern side of England, between the bulge of East Anglia to the east and the hillier parts of the Midlands to the west. The acreage was vast, a kind of English Zuider Zee of shallow waters and damp land, a wetland ranging in consistency from fully watery meres and rivers to soggy reedland and barely dry 'moors'. The fenland had made a frontier district between the old kingdoms of Mercia and Anglia. A few islands of higher ground (not much higher) historically rose clear of the waters, and most of those sheltered monastic communities which had grown up around the isolated sanctuaries of individual saints, who for one reason or another had sought shelter there. Of these, by far the biggest and also on what was historically the biggest island, is Ely, the island of eels, where the great cathedral still stands on a raised patch of ground above the flats.

This great wet landscape – it must have resembled the Danube delta or the Sologne more than the great arable plain we see now – became attractive to developers from the seventeenth century and their struggle with the waters became increasingly successful through the eighteenth and nineteenth centuries. They had the backing of the Crown, and the language that they used was always the language of 'improvement' of the land by drainage. The pioneering efforts of such as the seventeenth century Lord Bedford who employed Dutch engineers (Cornelius Vermuyden is routinely cited as the foremost among them) were only moderately successful because windmills could simply not pump enough water. The partial drainage allowed the peat to dry, and in drying it shrank and in shrinking its surface grew lower and still more liable to flood. But the classic patterns of the Industrial Revolution eventually applied to fenland drainage as much as to the draining of mines in Cornwall: as more powerful steam pumps became more common, so the industrial transformation could be accomplished. The huge land grab known as 'parliamentary enclosure' was to take place in the Fens as it was to take place everywhere else. Vast Fenland tracts today are still called the Bedford Levels, although the pumping is now done by electric pumps or diesel. The rivers are man-made or man-altered. Sea-walls and dykes and sluices need constant care. Draining the land also drains resources, but it's a necessary expense that underlies everything in this region. The whole area, by the way, is eminently vulnerable to climate change in the future.

So the drained landscape is new. It was arrived at not only by the technical means of the drains and the pumps, but at considerable social cost. There grew up, as there did elsewhere in the British Isles, a whole movement of resistance to 'improvement' and enclosure. There were Fen Tigers, soggy Luddites who breached embankments and smashed sluices. Some of their resistance literature survives, as for example the anonymous seventeenth century Powte's Complaint:

> Come, Brethren of the water, and let us all assemble,
> To treat upon this matter, which makes us quake and tremble;
> For we shall rue it, if't be true, that Fens be undertaken
> And where we feed in Fen and Reed, they'll feed both Beef and Bacon.
>
> They'll sow both beans and oats, where never man yet thought it,
> Where men did row in boats, ere undertakers brought it:
> But, Ceres, thou, behold us now, let wild oats be their venture,
> Oh let the frogs and miry bogs destroy where they do enter.
>
> Behold the great design, which they do now determine,
> Will make our bodies pine, a prey to crows and vermine:
> For they do mean all Fens to drain, and waters overmaster,
> All will be dry, and we must die, 'cause Essex calves want pasture.
> ......
> Wherefore let us intreat our ancient water nurses,
> To shew their power so great as t' help to drain their purses;
> And send us good old Captain Flood to lead us out to battle,
> Then two-penny Jack, with skales on's back, will drive out all the cattle.
>
> This noble Captain yet was never known to fail us,
> But did the conquest get of all that did assail us;
> His furious rage none could assuage; but, to the world's great wonder,
> He bears down banks, and breaks their cranks and whirlygigs asunder…[1]

The status of agricultural workers declined until in the nineteenth century they had changed from many-skilled graziers in summer and fowlers in winter, able to work reeds or trap eels, to simple 'hands' worked in gangs transported daily to huge monocrop fields.

There is plenty of evidence[2] that the consumption of opium was higher in the Fens than anywhere else in England. When the 1868 Pharmacy Act restricted its sale to specialist druggists, they were surprised in many Fenland towns by the vast quantities of opium they started to dispense which had previously been sold quite openly in grocers' stores. It was much used against the malarial agues particular to marshland; but beyond that, was more commonly used in the region as a sedative or palliative for children than elsewhere in England (which may well have a lot to do with the very high infant mortality rates recorded in the nineteenth century Fens). There seems also to have been some sense that opium dreams were a special antidote to the unrelieved flatness of the place. Thomas Hood, "was much surprised to find that opium or opic, as it was vulgarly called, was in quite common use in the form of pills among the lower class, in the vicinity of the Fens ... the Fen people in the dreary, foggy, cloggy, boggy wastes of Cambridge and Lincolnshire had flown to the drug for the sake of the magnificent scenery..."[3]

If the drug itself is only occasionally seen there, the melancholy tristesse which opium might have relieved is on every page of Graham Swift's *Waterland*. Here's a child's description of an old-time character, Bill Clay by name :

> "...a one-time punt-gunner and turf-cutter, who had witnessed in his lifetime the passing of all but the dregs of the old wild fens in our area; who stank, even with his livelihood half gone, of goose fat and fish slime, mud and peat smoke; who wore an otter-skin cap, eel-skin gaiters and whose brain was permanently crazed by the poppy-head tea he drank to ward off winter agues. Old Bill lived with his wife Martha in a damp, crack-walled cottage not far from the Ouse and on the edge of the shrinking, reed-filled marsh."[4]

There are very few people in these pictures; there are not so many smallholders of the Fens left. In photographic terms, they might have looked like the people of Emerson's Norfolk Broads, which are of a different geology but whose watery agriculture was in some regards parallel. Independent, highly skilled, 'quaint' only in that very specialized habits of husbandry had given rise to specialist tools – the reed rake, the punt gun, the high wader, the quant... There are photographers who chronicle just these lives as they have changed. I think above all of Justin Partyka, who has worked with wonderful sensitivity in agricultural communities in fenland as well as the slightly higher country further east in Norfolk and Suffolk. Years ago, I remember reviewing and very much liking Patrick Sutherland and Adam Nicholson's book on the Somerset Levels[5], a quite similar region of floodable low ground sandwiched between the Quantocks, the Mendips, and the Blackdown Hills on the other side of the country. Patrick Sutherland was more interested in pointing his camera at the people, in seeing their skills, in noting the harshness of a life apparently out of time, than Paul Hart seems to be. But I'm not at all sure that we should slip into the easy, lazy tramlines of conventional photographic thinking for that reason alone. Sutherland and Partyka have been interested in the way people live. Hart is more interested in the formal construction of the land in the velvety tones he conjures in his darkroom. Does that make the pictures of the former two somehow 'political' pictures, while depriving Hart of that 'seriousness' the label implies? Does his slow weighty glance stop us from thinking of Hart also as a documentarian, or even noticing that he, too, tells the truth? It should not.

These pictures, for all that extraordinary formal elegance, for all their self-conscious enjoyment of graphic balances, are not neutral. England is more or less entirely man-made. We know from great classics such as *The Making of the English Landscape*[6] a little of how to untangle the palimpsests that it presents. In places such as the Fens, where the drains are straight and the rivers are often embanked above the level of the surrounding ground, it is easy to see that man has been at his work, assiduously. That work is itself a political object, as Georgian London is or the great estates of the North. For some photographers, that is itself somehow the subject of what they do. When John Davies photographed the Durham coalfields in 1983 and toured the pictures extensively during the Miners' Strike, it was obvious that the wonderful darkroom skills, the elegance and harmony of the pictures were somehow subservient to the messaging, the beautiful rendering of all that might be lost, or had already been lost. When Simon Roberts looked at the leisure gatherings of the English in a generation where work was getting scarcer and taking less time, and the world was filling up with days-out and days-off, we felt the same again, that the beautiful sensitive manner of making the pictures was subservient to the messaging. Davies was from County Durham: we knew that we were expected to think that his view was sympathetic to the great tribe of coal miners, then under sustained attack. Roberts had a degree in human geography – we knew that his was a *study* as well as a collection of views.

The fact that the social and political upheaval in the Fens took place a couple of hundred years ago doesn't allow us to think that the place is now socially and politically inert, or that a person photographing there is only interested in the shape of the dykes and the breadth of the sky over the flatlands.

It is a long and rich tradition in Britain — and one into which Paul Hart fits perfectly — which regards the land itself as a specifically political document while not necessarily approaching it in openly political terms. The photographer Edwin Smith did exactly that. So did Paul Hill once he'd moved away from his first career as a reporter. Paul Graham most certainly did. Joseph Koudelka — who has photographed a great deal in Wales even though he plainly cannot count as a British photographer — is a most wonderful photographer of the land in his later incarnation as a specialist panoramic photographer; but never at the expense of the politics which the land makes visible. In each case, the strictly personal appreciation of place, the simple idea that a photographer might be content to be somewhere, eyes open and sensibilities alert, is compounded by the layers of history which made that place what it is. The best example is Fay Godwin, for whom the ghosts of what a place had been were never absent from what it was on the day she was there. Fay Godwin often photographed places which had lost most of their importance. Former industrial sites, abandoned routes, places of the worship of gods we no longer acknowledge. In each case, Godwin found ways to let the ghosts speak, but without overwhelming the simple geographical volumes of the place where she found them. Godwin, in other words, like those others, was a political photographer even when she wasn't overtly photographing political effects. Godwin may well have learnt to do this from one particular source, Bill Brandt's *Literary Britain*. Hers was, after all, a particularly literary career. Her husband had been a distinguished editor (Tony Godwin, who contributed many important changes to Penguin Books) and her initial work was producing portraits of literary figures.

Later she worked with many great writers in partnership. The ghosts, in other words, could be imaginary as much as historical. Brandt's great *Top Withens* is loaded from fiction, not specially from fact.

That's counter-intuitive if you happened to grow up thinking there was something called 'documentary' (or 'concerned photography', as a sub-set of it was called at one time in the UK) which was somehow distinct from 'landscape' and in opposition to it. But they don't have to be separate. Keith Arnatt's *Area of Outstanding Natural Beauty*, Paul Nash's incredible studies of Maiden Castle in Dorset, even Donovan Wylie's *Watchtowers* – so many different kinds of pictures take elements from the romantic view of the landscape and blend them in their own proportions with elements taken from the scrutiny of (or the anxiety for) the social. The British landscape is itself a political document.[7]

The pictures in *Drained* follow naturally from Hart's previous book, which was called *Farmed* and which concentrated more upon the economic activity of the place. Together they make a description of that Fenland landscape which contains elements of the story of the place as well as its lineaments. Electricity and water and trains and cars all run more or less straight in that part of the world. They all run from out of the picture, through it, then out again. It's as though there's no reason to stop anywhere rather than anywhere else. Why stop here? A stand of trees. A blinded house or chapel, hardly used. The economic activity here is in the mud, the amazingly fertile mud, and for most days of the year it just needs to be left to itself. Then there'll be a lot of noise and bustle, and a load of cabbages will be lifted in a day, and silence will descend on the mud again. The National Farmers' Union produced a set of statistics to say that about half of all Grade 1 land in England is in the Fens, and the area produces 37% of all the vegetables produced here[8]. This is a major industrial habitat, although it doesn't look like a Lowry.

Paul Hart is a photographer interested in the slow harvesting of hidden truth from the ordinary places that most of us pass by. He works in an unfashionable idiom with slow cumbrous equipment (not just old-fashioned analogue photography, but medium format analogue photography, slower still) in an unfashionable place. He seeks to find the bits of the land that speak their stories, and to transmit their importance in views in which, typically, the absolute lack of melodrama demands slow looking and brings slow revelation. Hart's placid, formally peaceful landscape is pregnant with stories that lurk in the mud or the mist. His magic lies in soliciting from his viewers the same half-historical, half-romantic reaction to ploughed fields and straight drainage ditches as he has to them himself.

It is routine to describe pictures of flat fields (often foggy) as sad. There is melancholy and enough to go around in these pages, to be sure. Part of the sadness lies in the sheer waste that they remind us of. It's not just that reed-cutters lost their jobs when the reed-beds were drained. It's also that food waste is itself a huge problem, especially in developed countries, and more especially in the fruit and veg sector to which the Fens are largely given. Even without statistics, we know that a proportion of everything we see grown on these pages is simply thrown away. All the same, simply to badge this landscape as sad and then turn away won't quite do. The big barn at Streetway is not a picturesque ruin merely waiting for passing photographers to seize it as it tumbles down. It's been carefully repaired, although it was maybe too expensive to reproduce those lovely triangular wedges of angled courses that make the gable. (I've seen those described as *vlechtingen* courses – braiding or plaited courses – and they're certainly more common in the Netherlands than in England.) That barn is still a working place. The young man leading a horse away on a bike is not doing it for picturesque reasons. There's maintenance and care in every picture – this is almost a gardened landscape. Pollarding doesn't just do itself. Uncleared drains don't drain. A construction like the tumbledown galvanised building at Cut End Road does represent change; but it may be wrong to think of it first as *sad*. Would you really like to have lived there? If you had a car, even a cheap car, wouldn't you prefer to live in Fishtoft, on the edge of Boston, just the other side of the Hobhole Drain?

These places of scattered settlement and sparse population don't exactly look like the sites of an industrial revolution, and the level plains of timeless-looking mud upon which they sit don't quite look like a brand-new land. But in the Fens, the world keeps on changing. It's up to us to see the new patterns of labour in these fields, whereby poorly-protected field hands – often East Europeans on seasonal contracts – work so arduously to preserve the illusion of 'country farming' apparently necessary to the customers of Waitrose or Morrisons. Competition means that vegetable prices simply cannot be allowed to rise high enough to make decent wages standard all the way down the production chain. You see a boarded-up house behind its windbreak of fast-growing trees in *Oldfield Lane*, with its long-silent burglar alarm positioned to be as visible from the lane as possible? It wasn't run-of-the-mill burglars who despoiled that place. That's called 'shifting patterns of rural employment' – but it takes away people's goods with the same certainty.

It is not just my imagination that sees a trench in *Leverton Lucasgate* or *Mill Drain* and finds uncomfortable echoes of Passchendaele in Hart's *Station Farm* or *New Marsh*.

> There shall be
> In that rich earth a richer dust concealed;
> A dust whom England bore, shaped, made aware …[9]

The resemblance to the Flanders fields of Great War poetry is not at all coincidental. In England, those flat lands have not been soused in blood in quite the same way as in Flanders. Yet the presence of a fortified bunker hints at the obvious: it might many times, had things been only slightly different, have been just as suitable a battleground as the one over the sea. The airfields like the one at Wainfleet which pepper the flatlands offered defense to the rest of England, but they certainly also needed defending themselves. This flat fertile country, so different to the hedge-punctuated rolling land we think of more typically, is still heartland-English, even though bits of it are called 'Holland' and tourists now come to be amazed at how 'other' the whole place looks. Fenland has held for generations people whose way of life did not in the end resist the steam pump or the computerised harvest. They didn't succumb to the mechanical maelstrom of carnage that we know in Flanders but to a slower atrophy. In Fenland was something barely known to outsiders, that now is no longer. There has been change in this landscape ever since it was drained. It is not just the shapes of the willows and poplars and the glint of the rain on scratchy tarmac that Paul Hart photographs so elegiacally. There are ghosts in these polders, too.

NOTES

1. Quoted in William Dugdale's 1662 history of the Draining of the Fens. For discussion on this remarkable poem cf. Borlik, Todd Andrew and Clare Egan, *Angling for the Powte: The Authorship, Provenance, and Manuscripts of a Jacobean Environmental Protest Poem*. English Literary Renaissance. ISSN 0013-8312, 2016
2. Virginia Berridge and Griffith Edwards, *Opium and the People, Opiate Use in Nineteenth-Century England*, Chapter 4, Opium in the Fens (New Haven, Yale University Press, 1987)
3. T. Hood, *Reminiscences*, quoted in H. A. Page, *Thomas De Quincey His Life and Writings* (London, John Hogg, 1877), pp. 233-4
4. Graham Swift, *Waterland* (London, Picador, 1996)
5. Adam Nicholson and Patrick Sutherland, *Wetland: Life in the Somerset Levels* (London, Michael Joseph, 1986)
6. Hoskins, W. G. *The Making of the English Landscape* (London: Hodder and Stoughton, 1956)
7. For one among many interesting discussions about how these elements can recombine in many different ways, see John Kippin, *Material Memories*; A Conference Presentation Delivered at the University of Newcastle 2015 and published in *The Post-Industrial Landscape as Site for Creative Practice*, edited by Gwen Heeney, (Cambridge Scholars Publishing, 2017). There was a good exhibition at the Towner Art Gallery in Eastbourne in late 2017 which looked at many of the same issues, too – and there are many other places to look.
8. NFU brochure : *Why Farming Matters in the Fens*, accessed as https://www.nfuonline.com/assets/23991, April 2018
9. Rupert Brooke, *The Soldier*, 1914

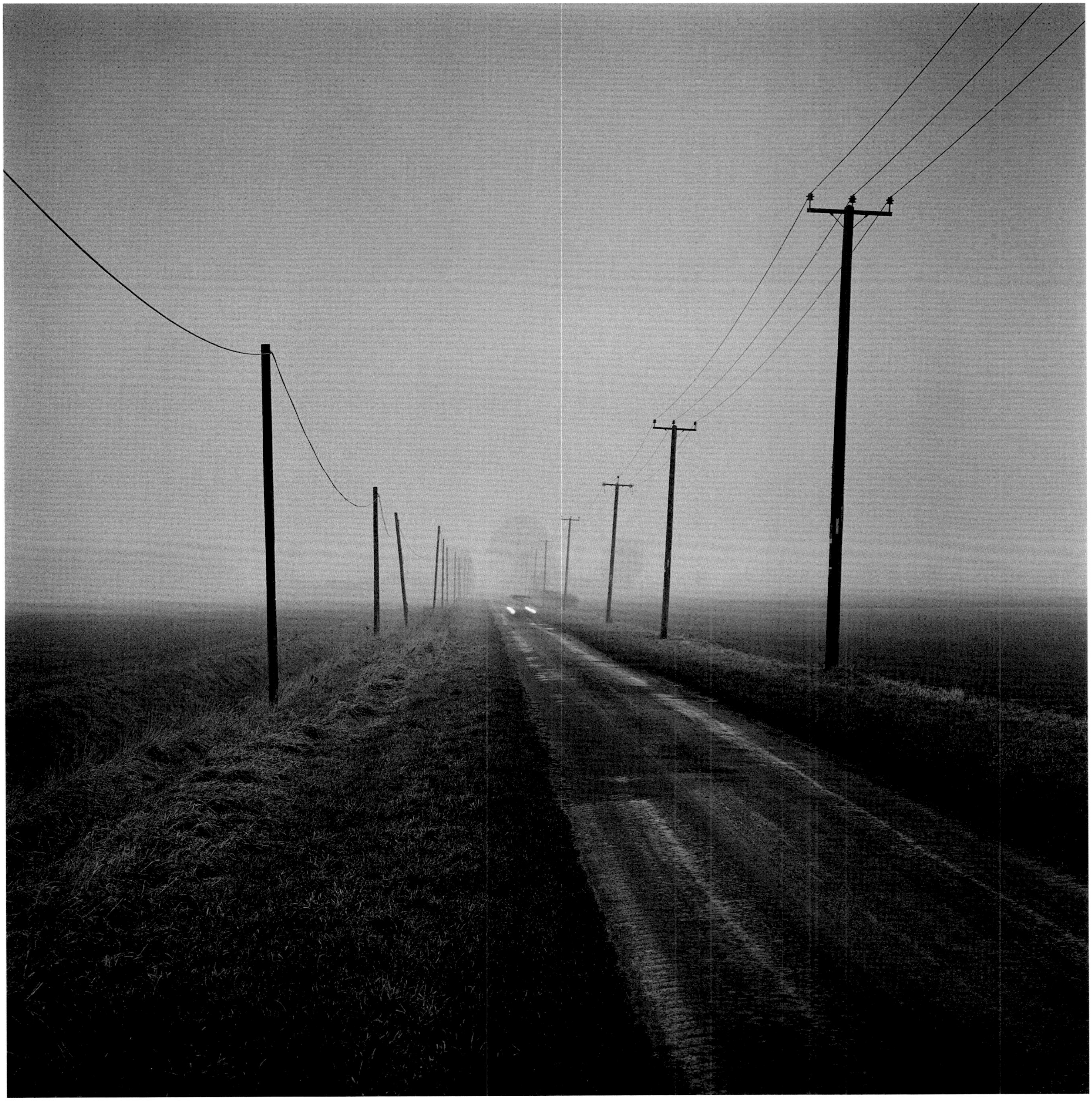

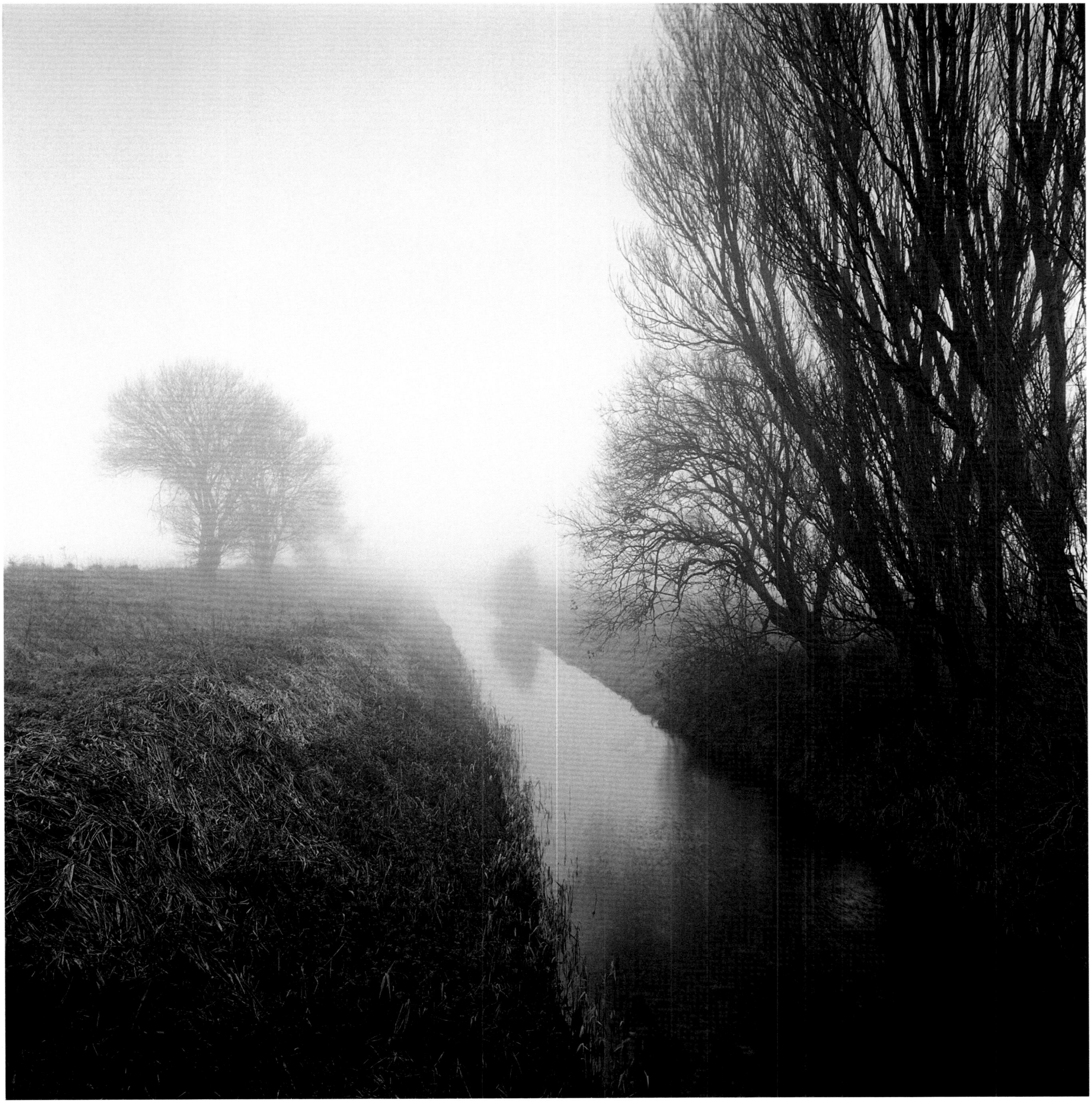

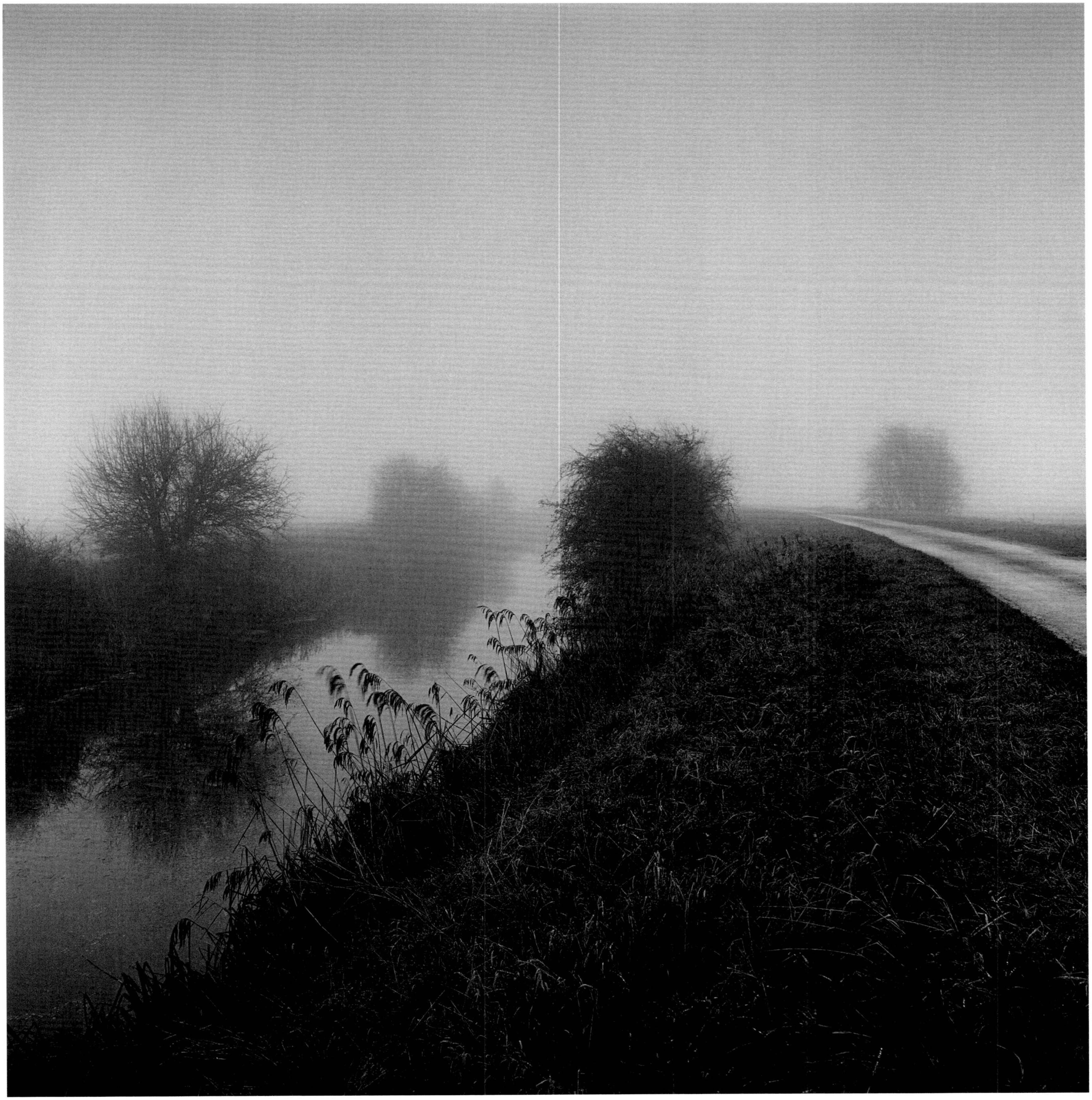

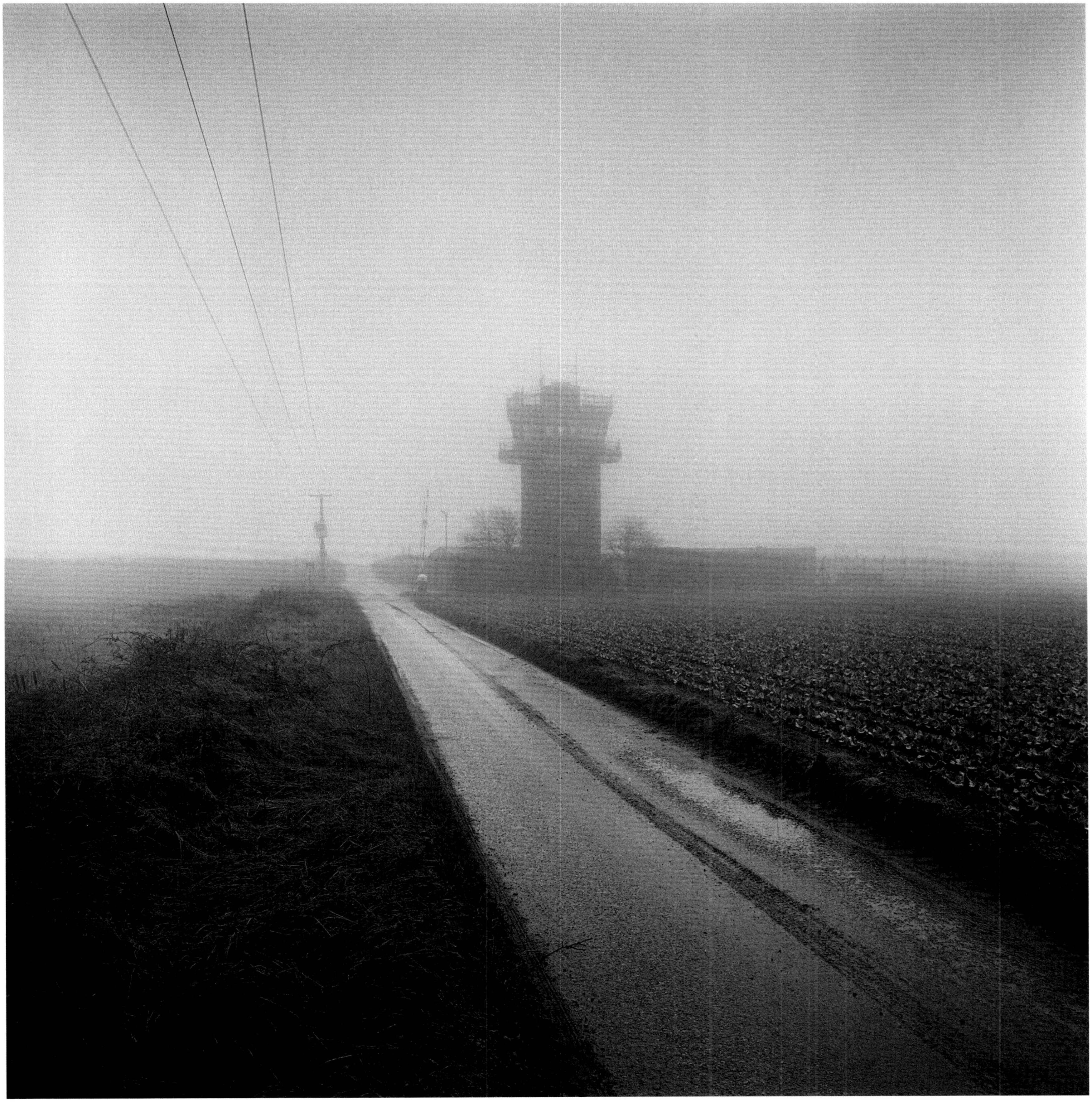

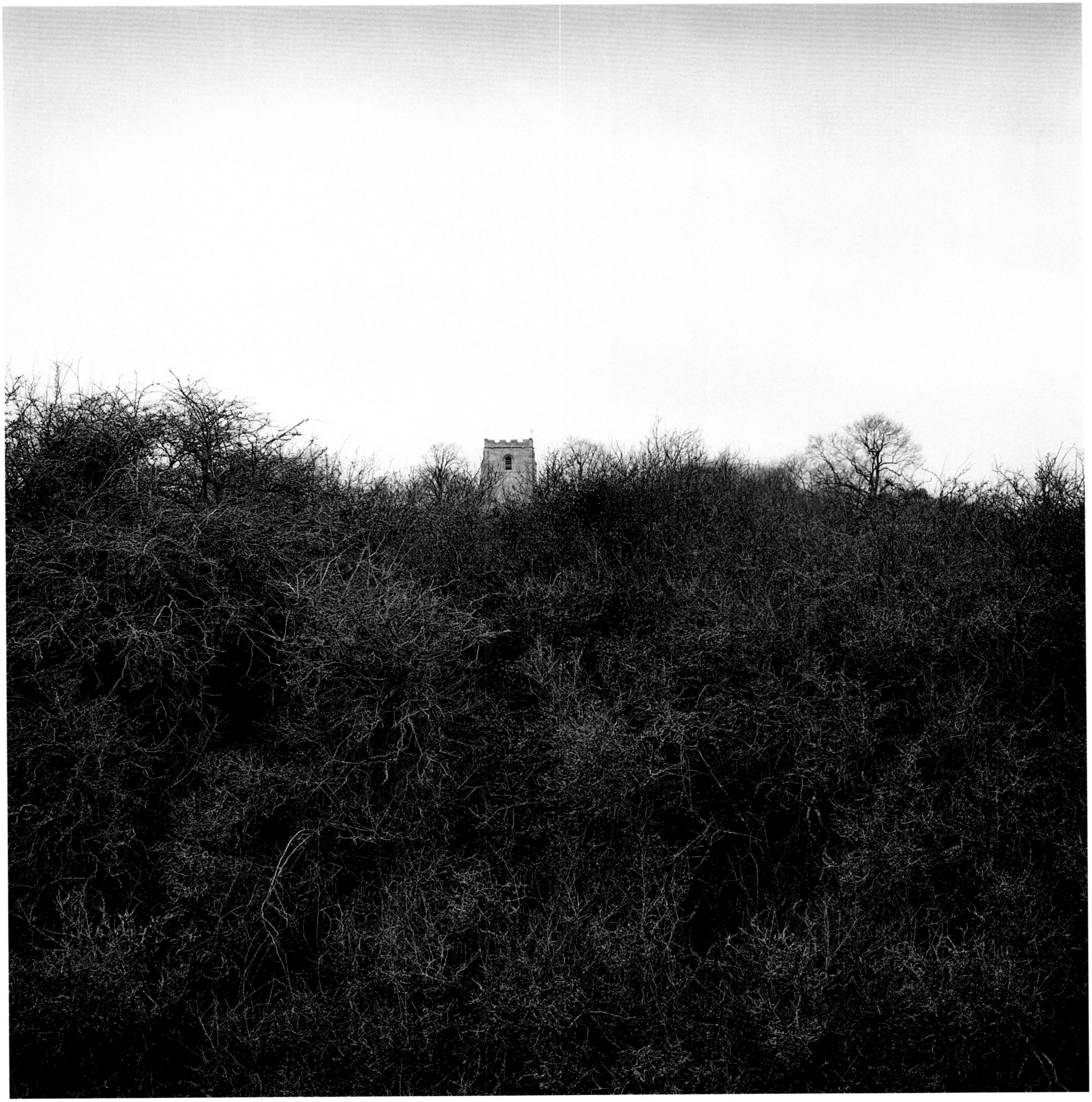

following pages: FREISTON SHORE | BLACK DROVE

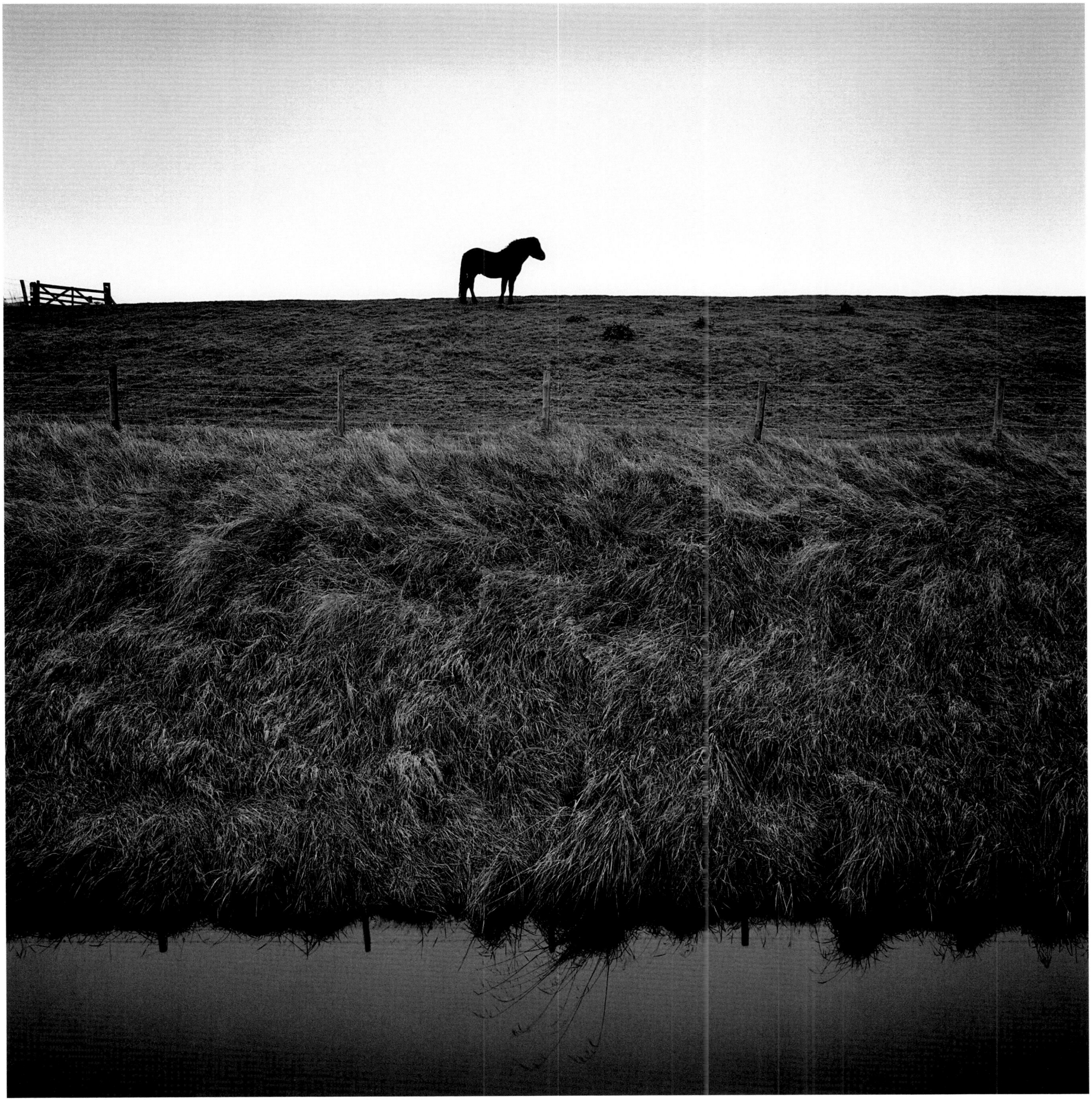

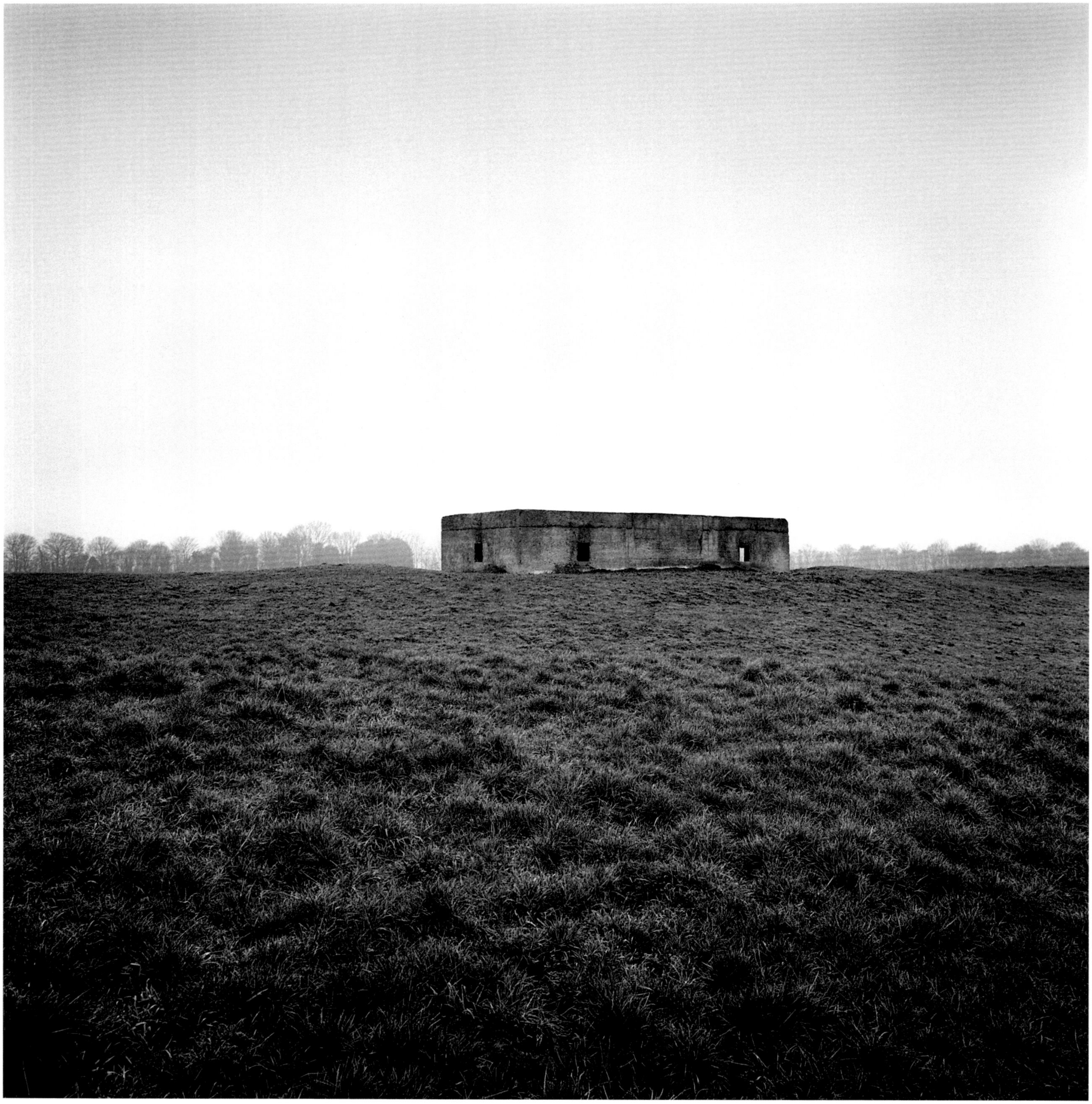

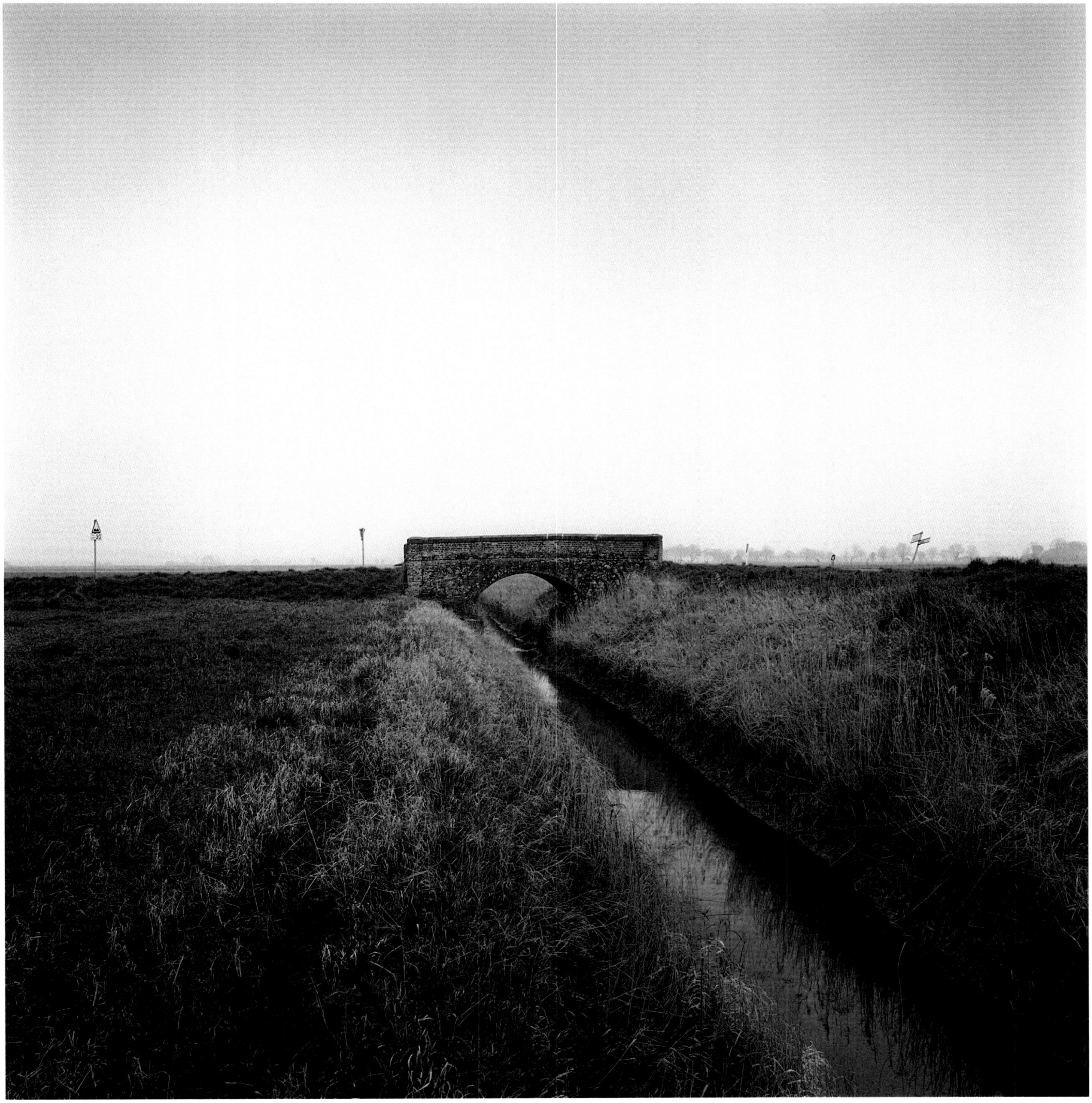

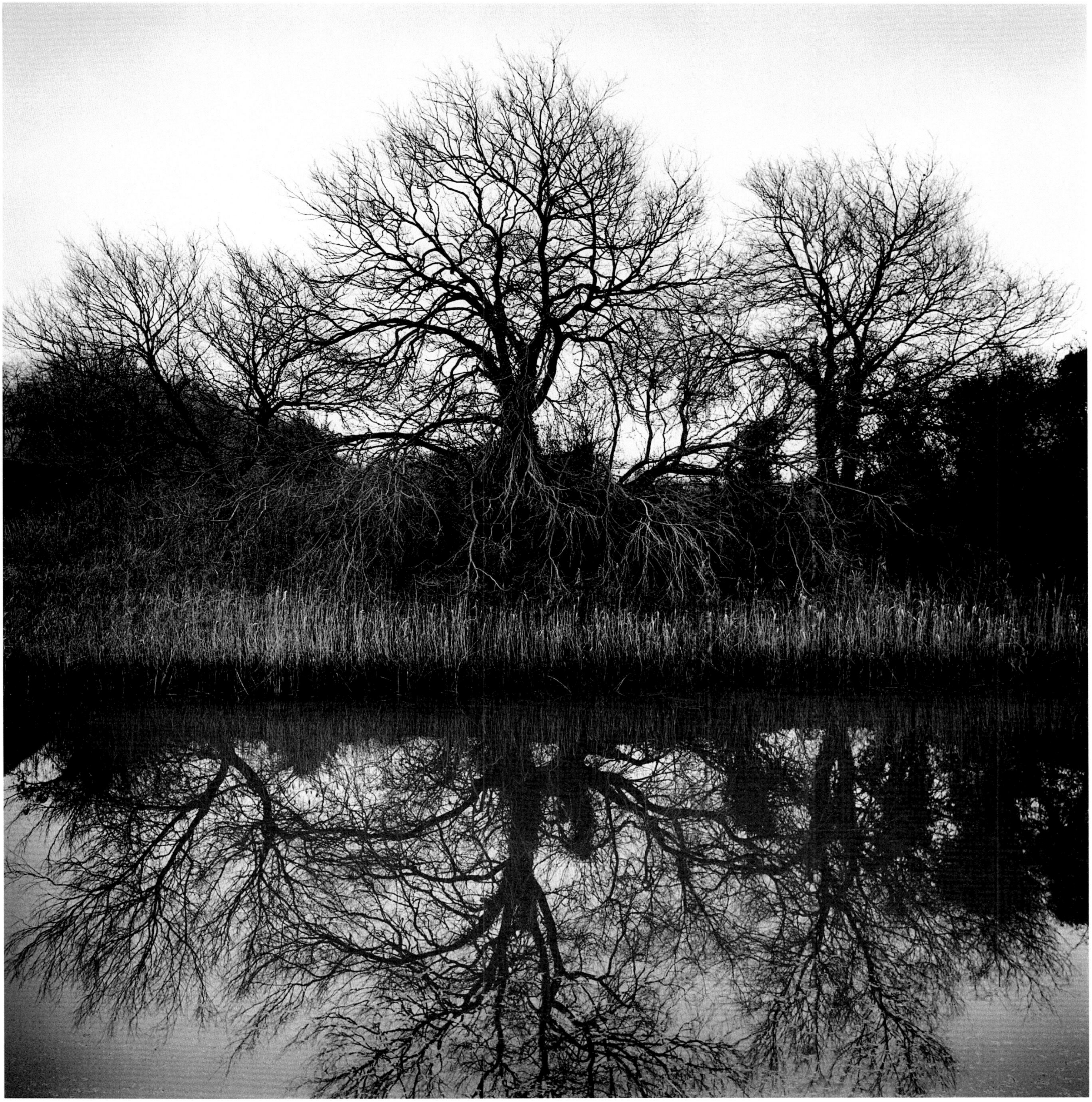

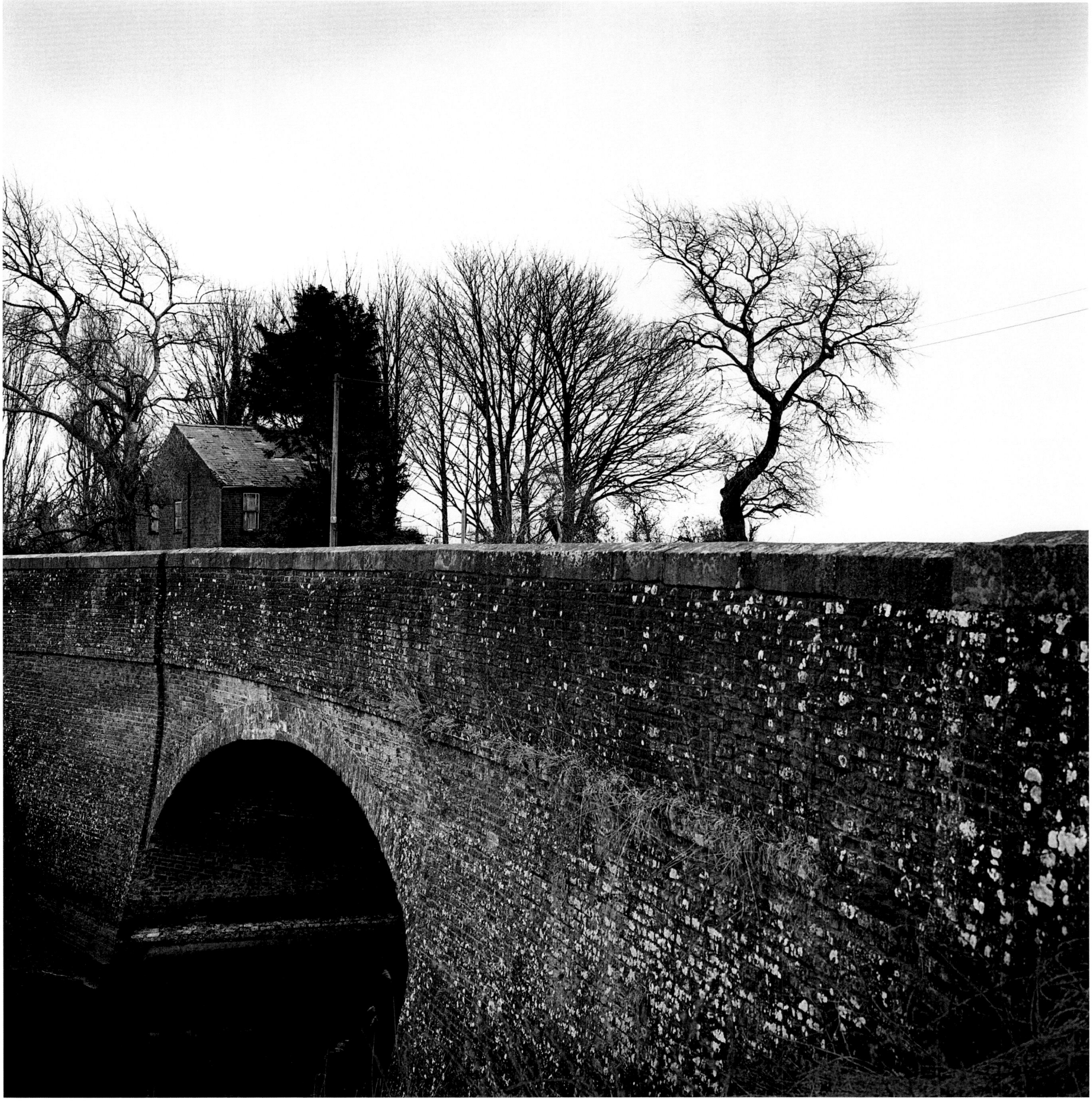

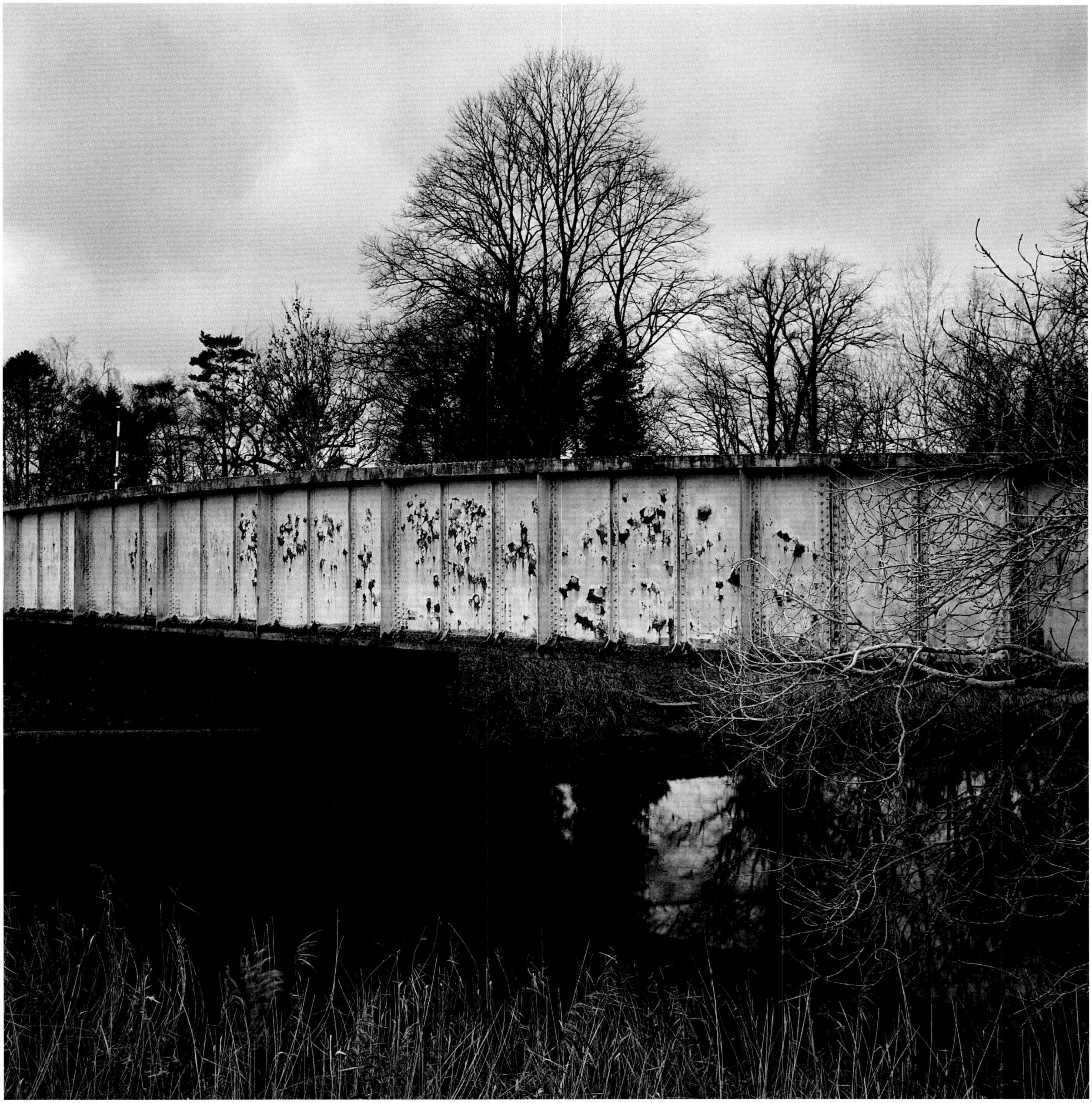

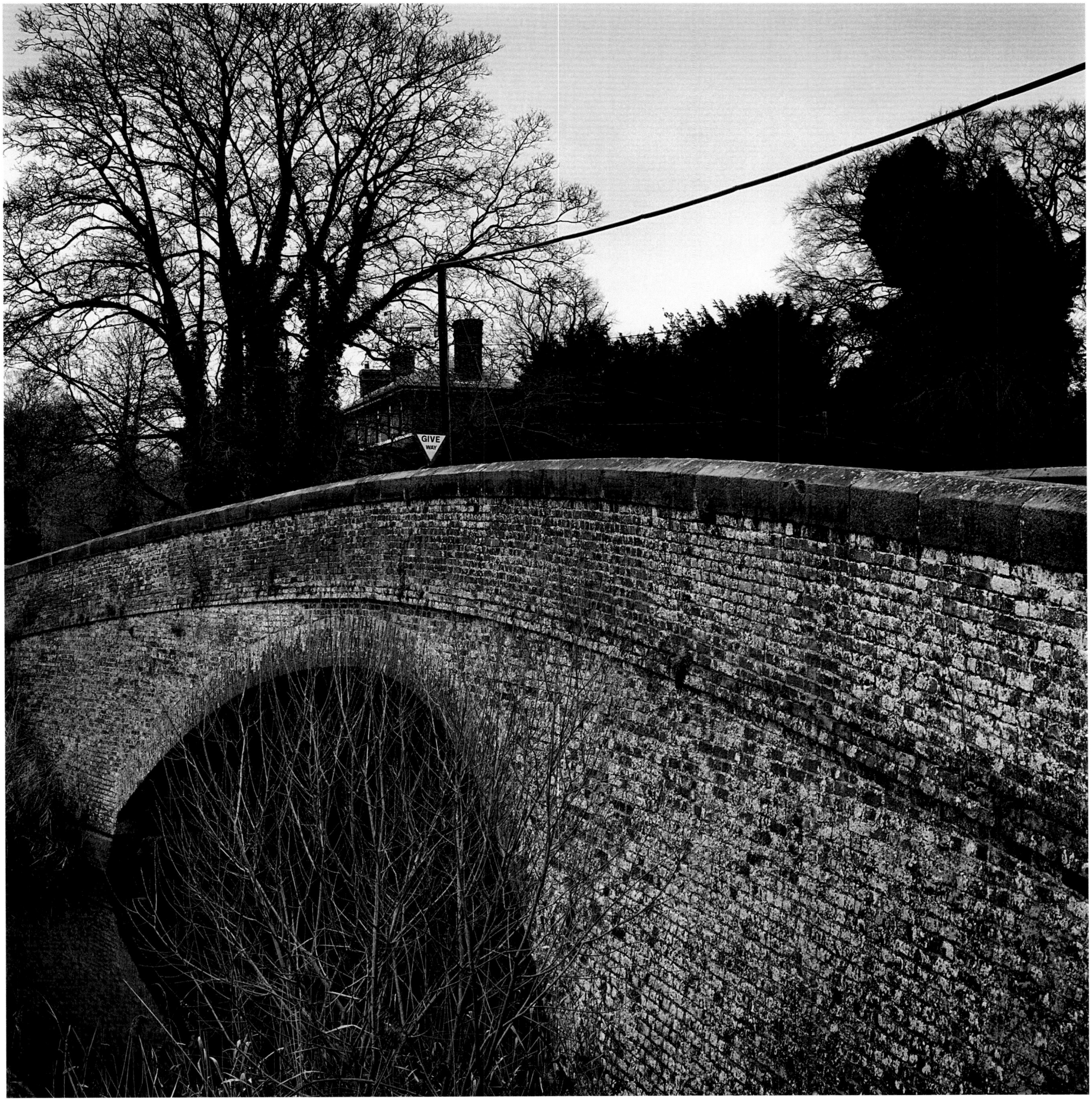
GIVE
WAY

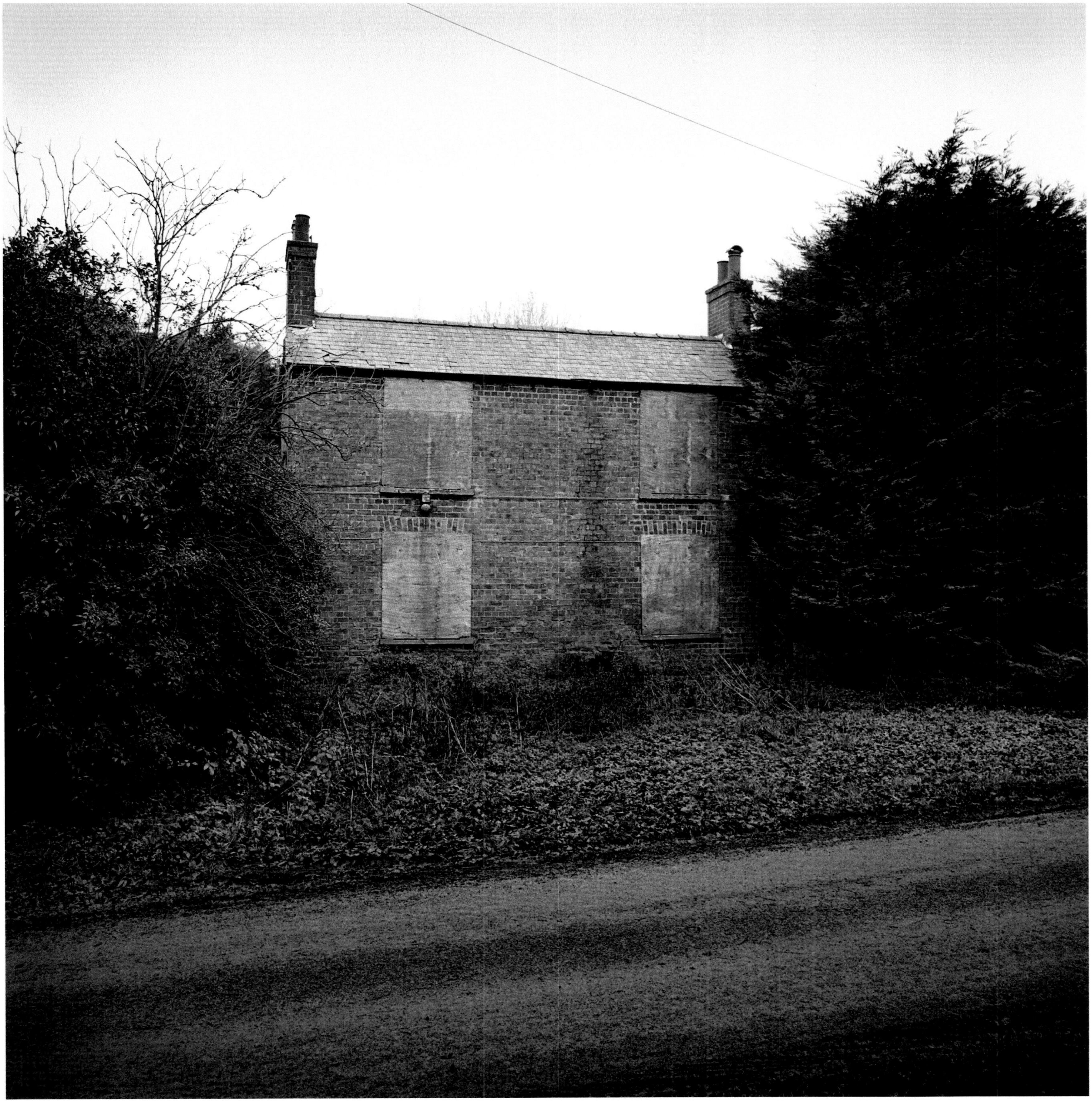

40 | BROTHERTOFT

following pages: FREISTON INGS | WYBERTON ROADS

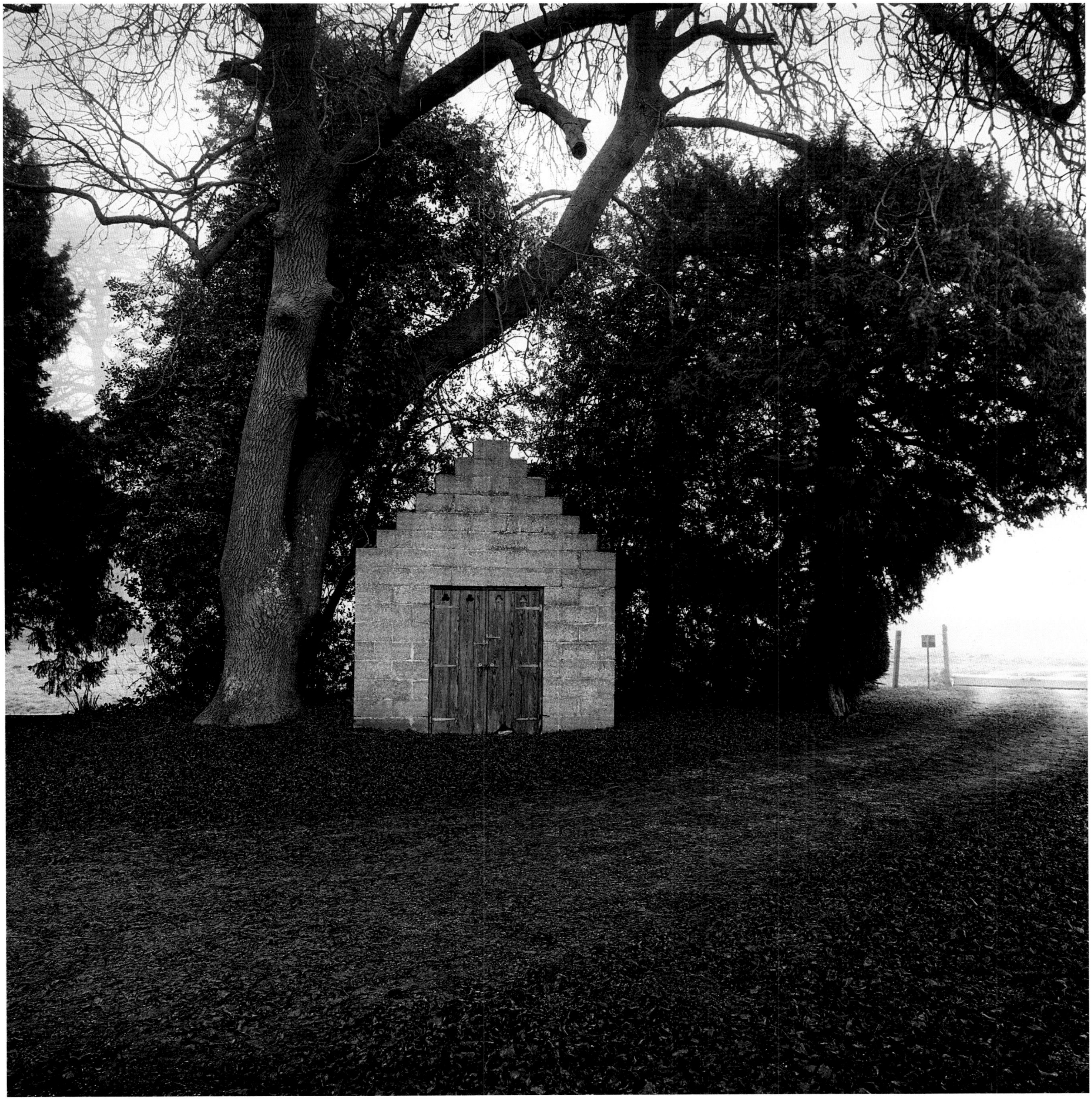

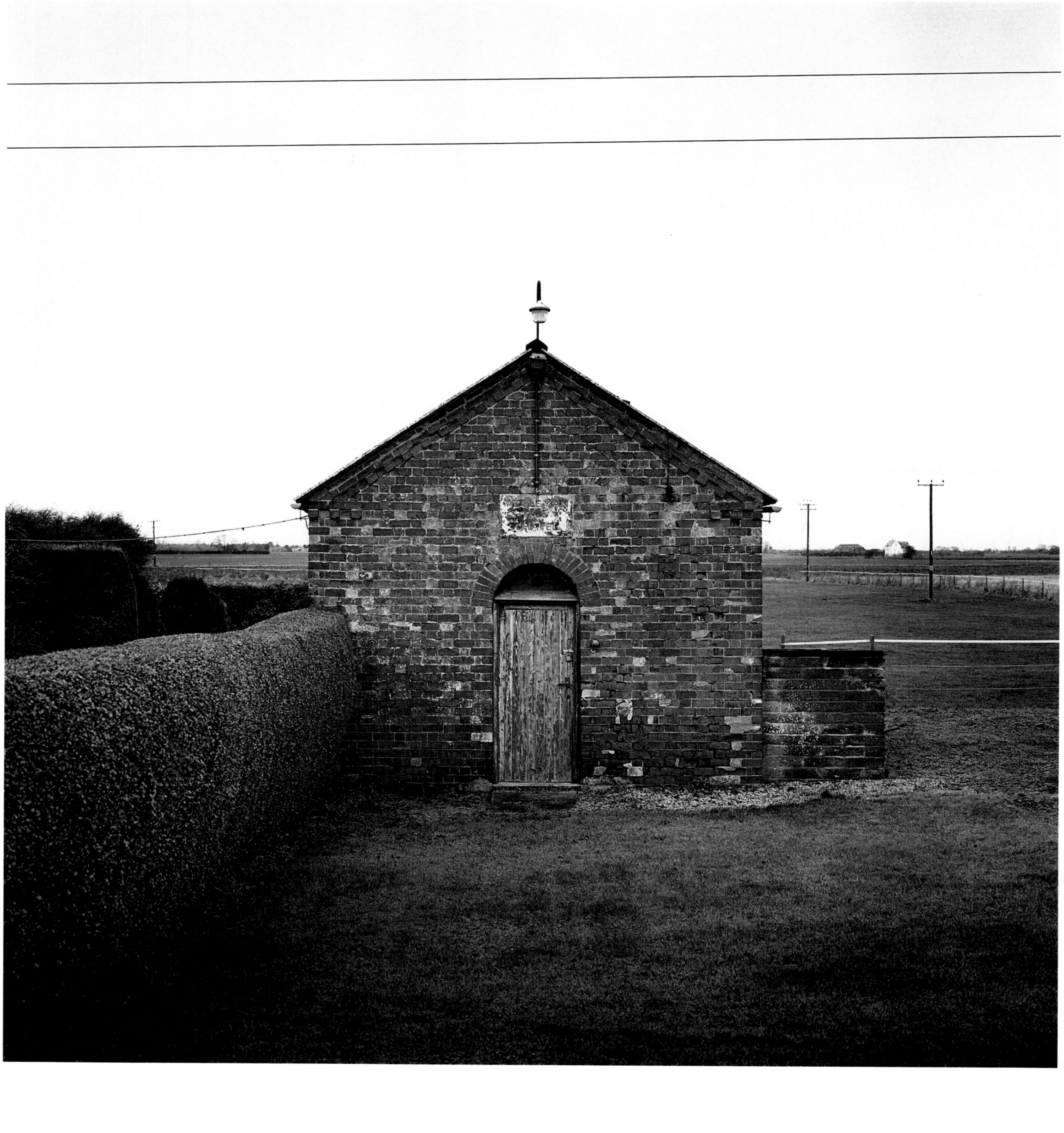

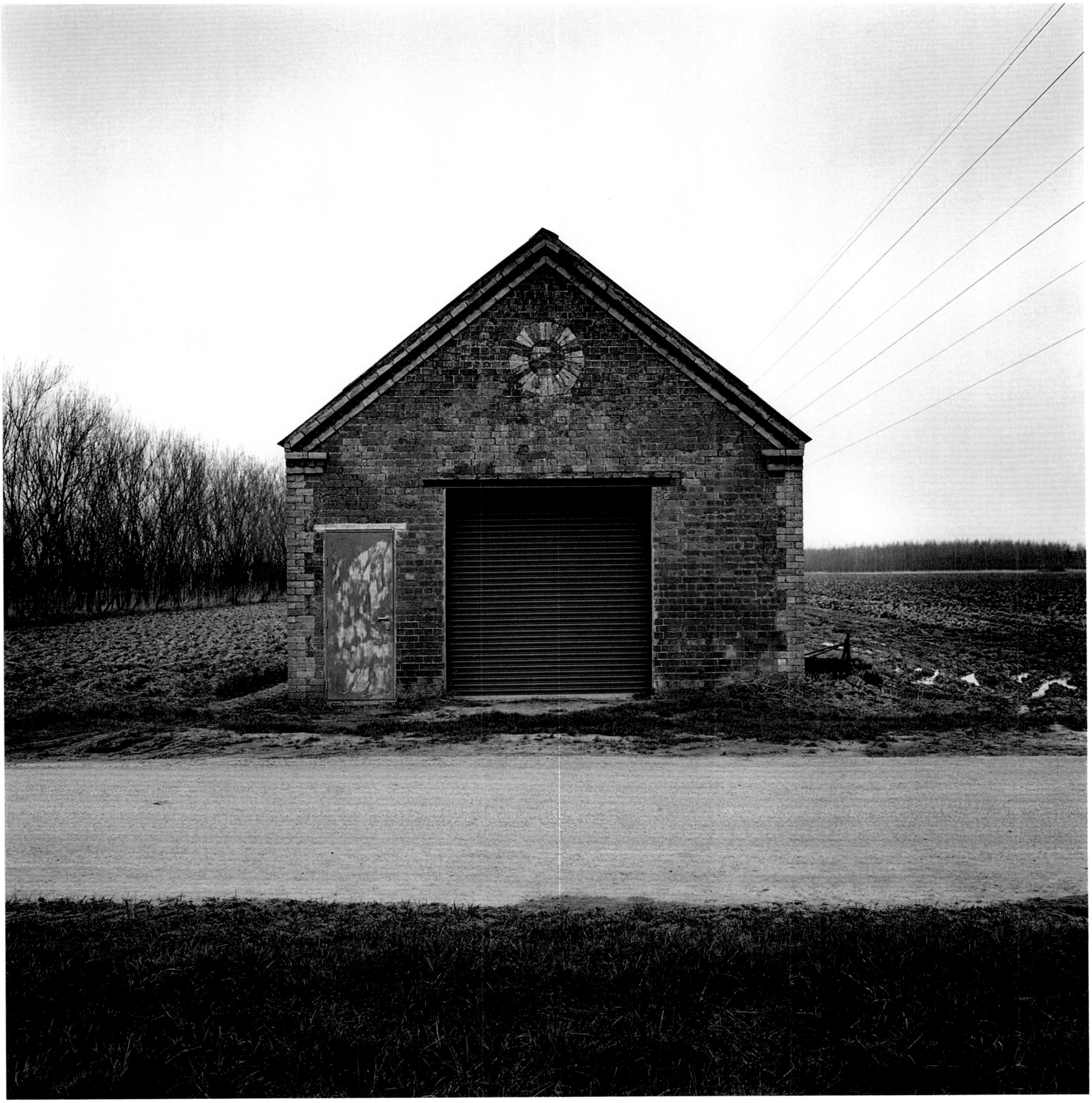

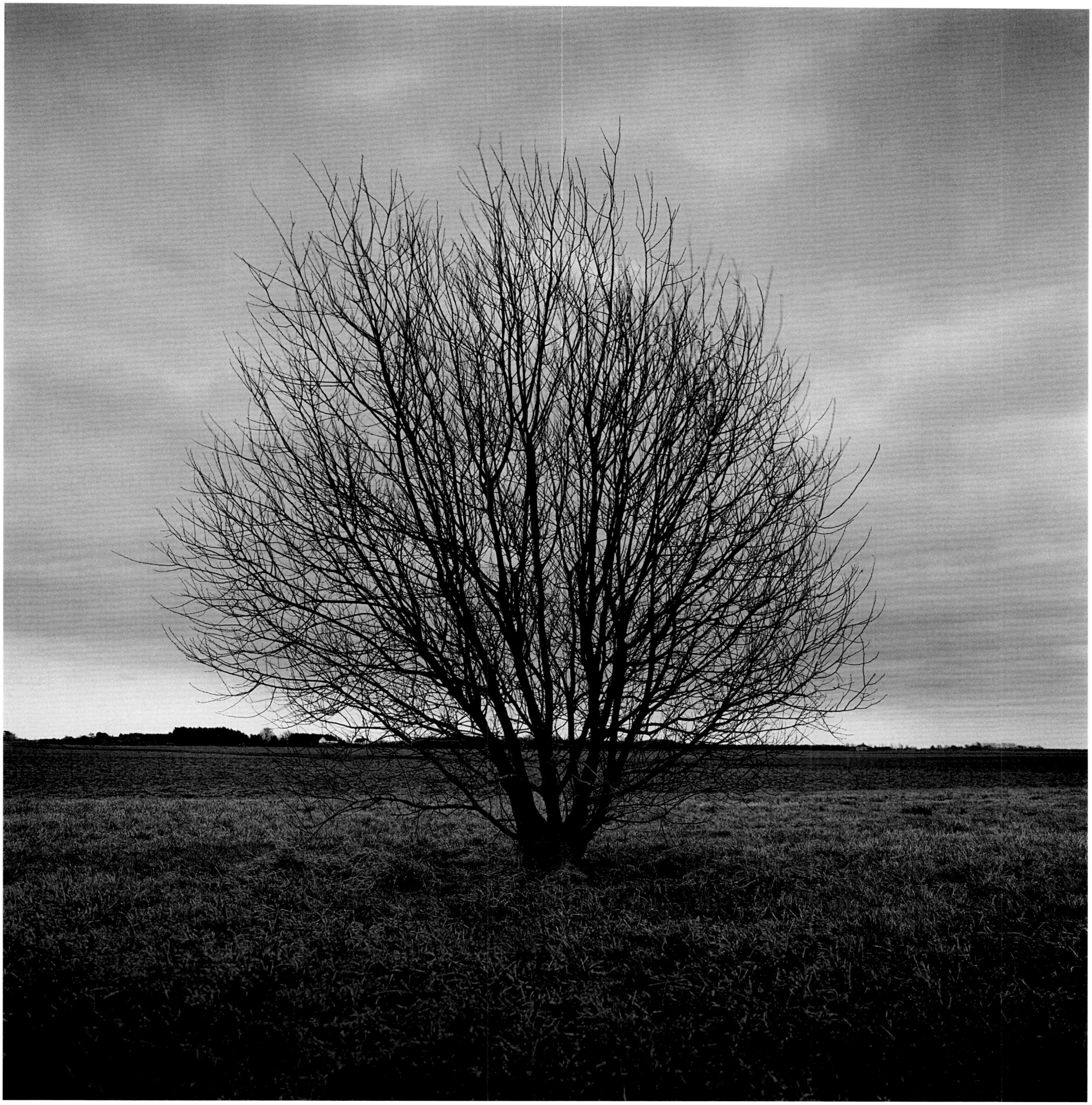

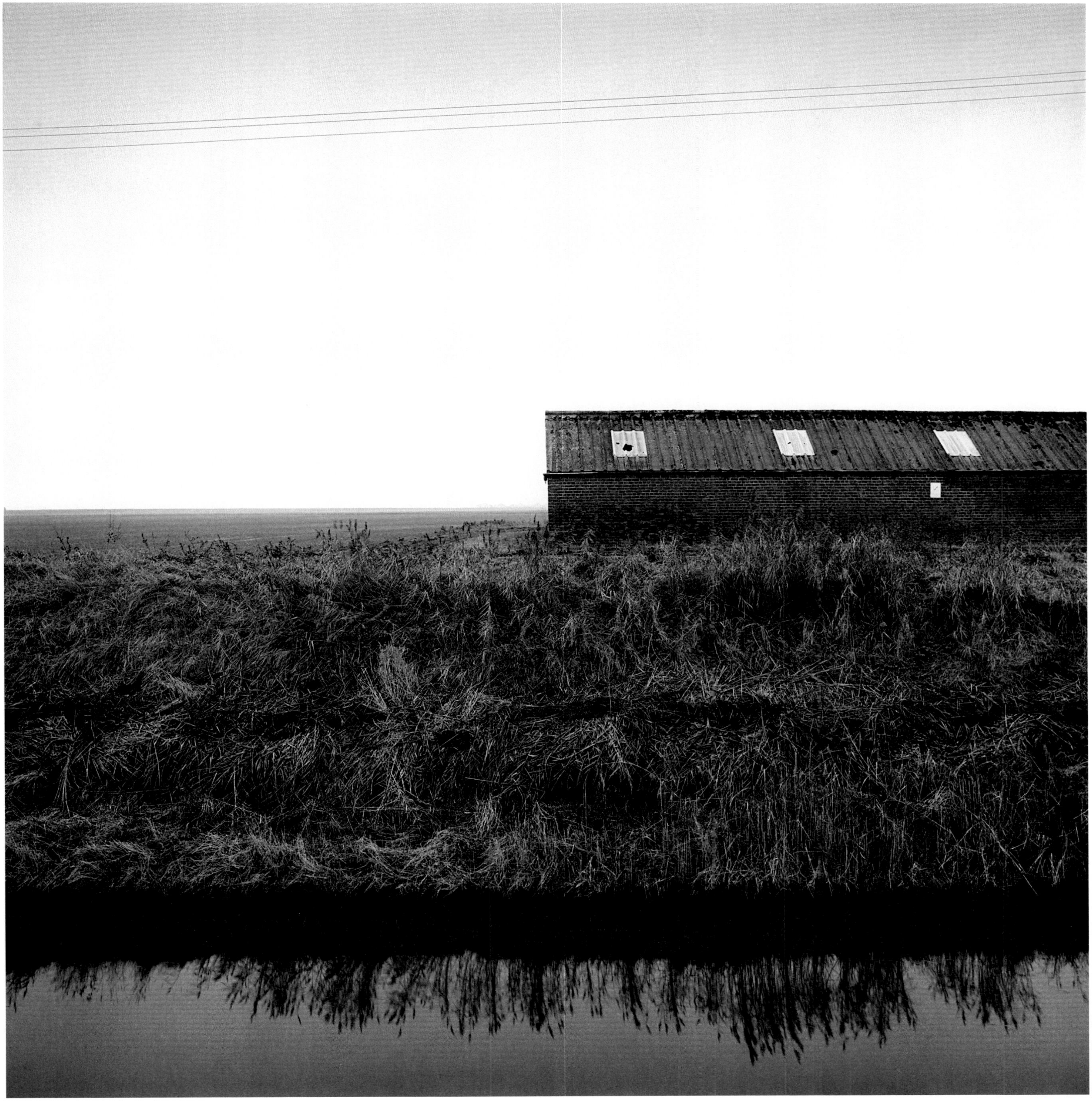

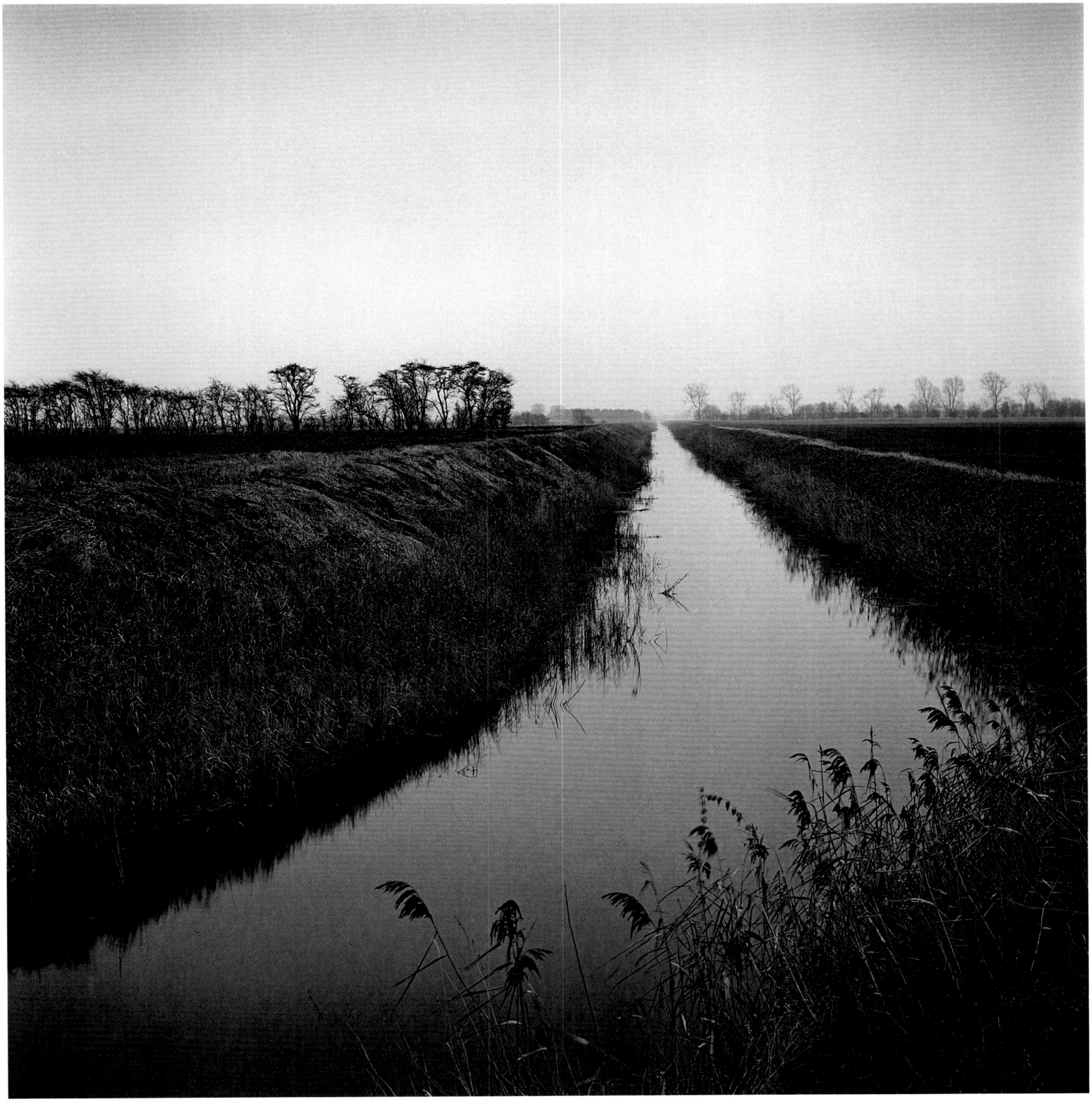

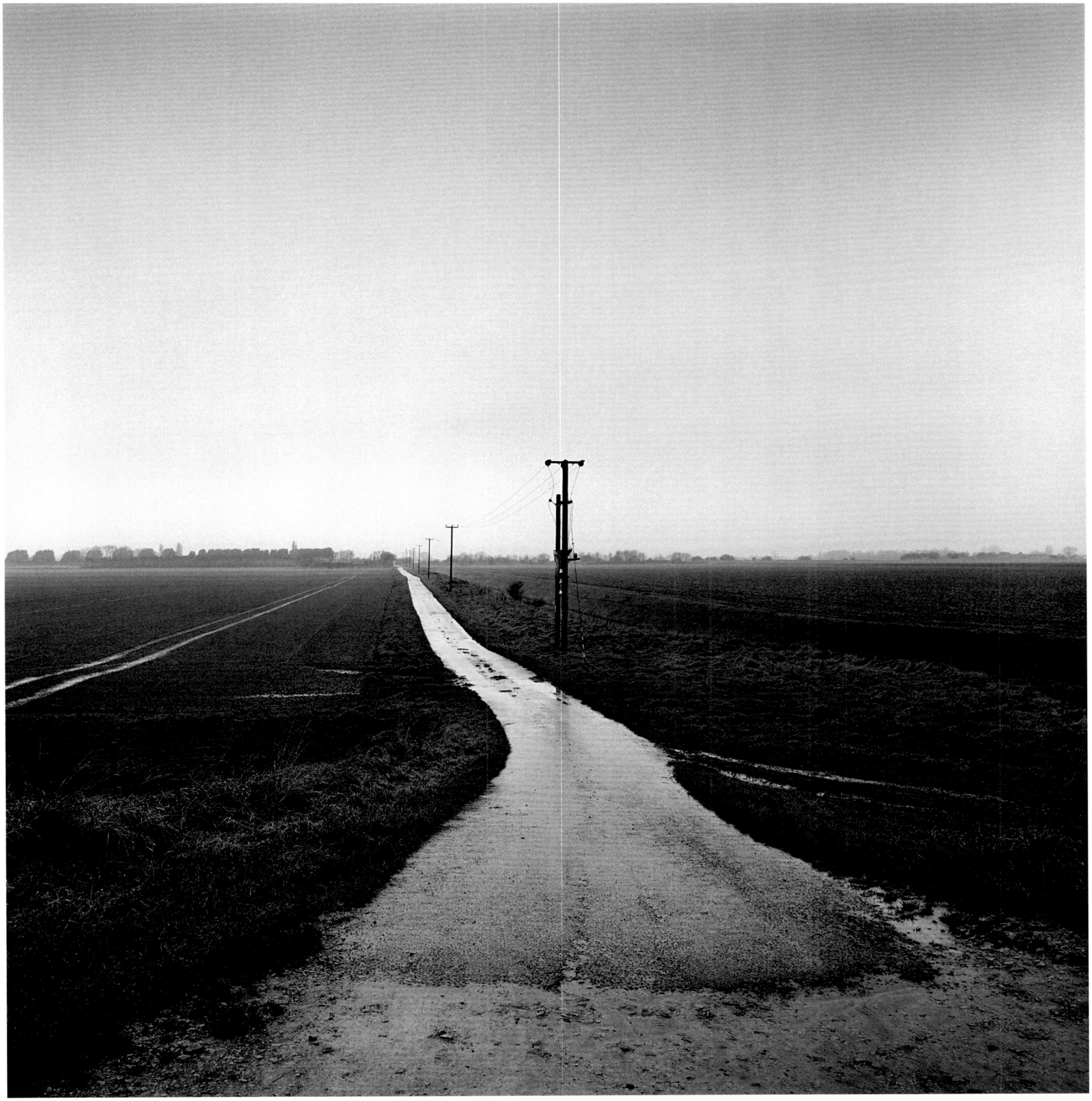

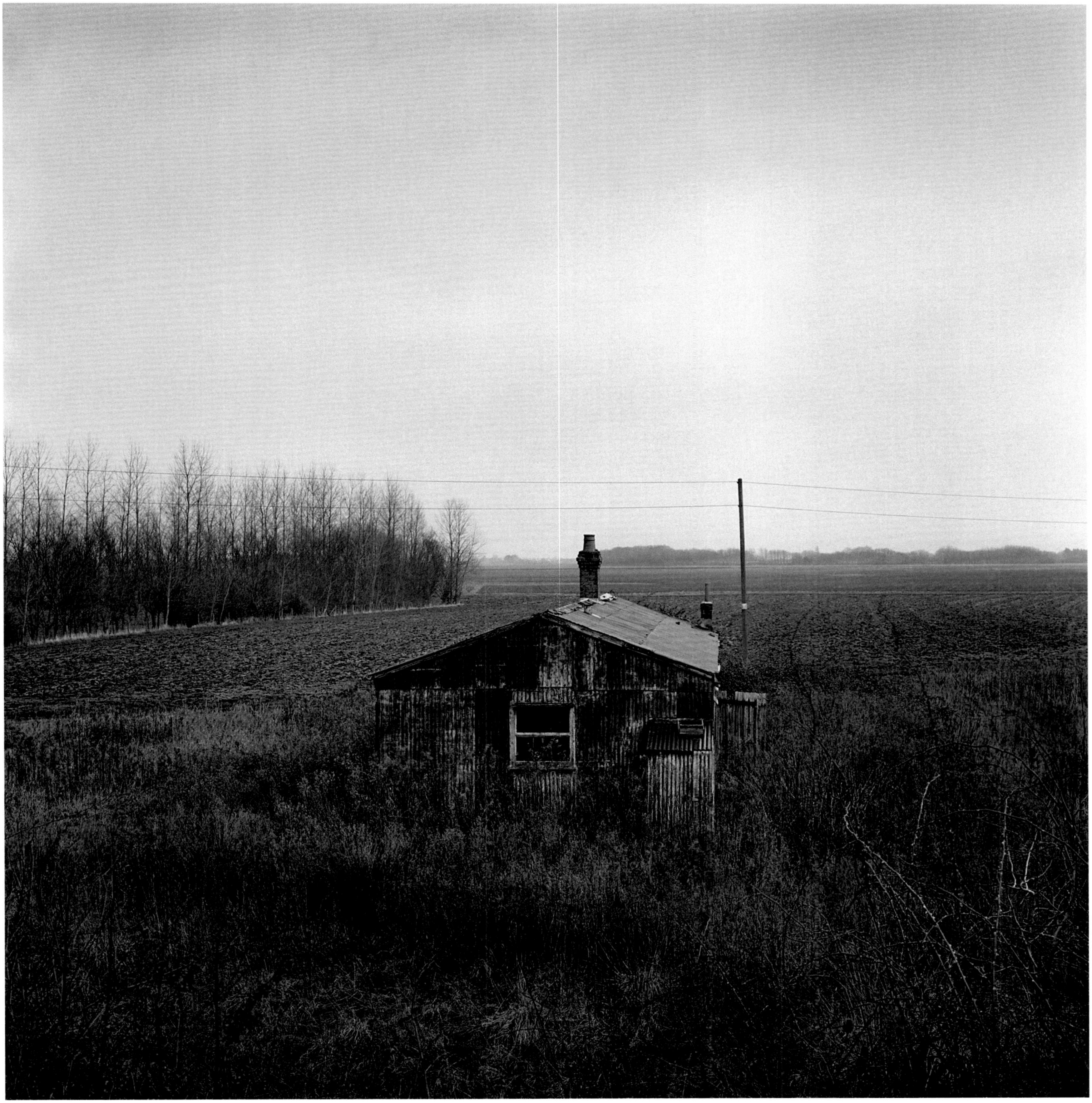

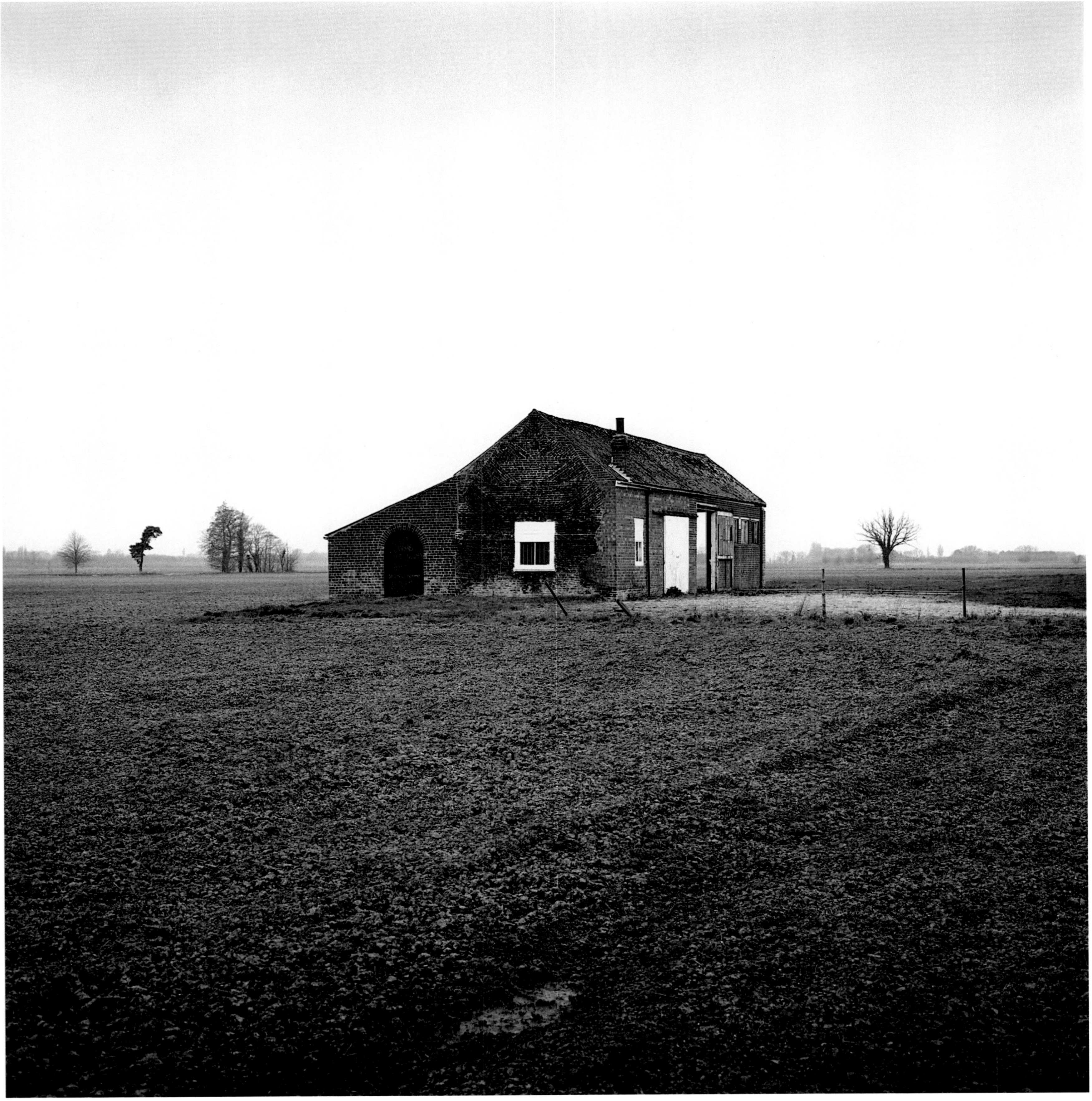

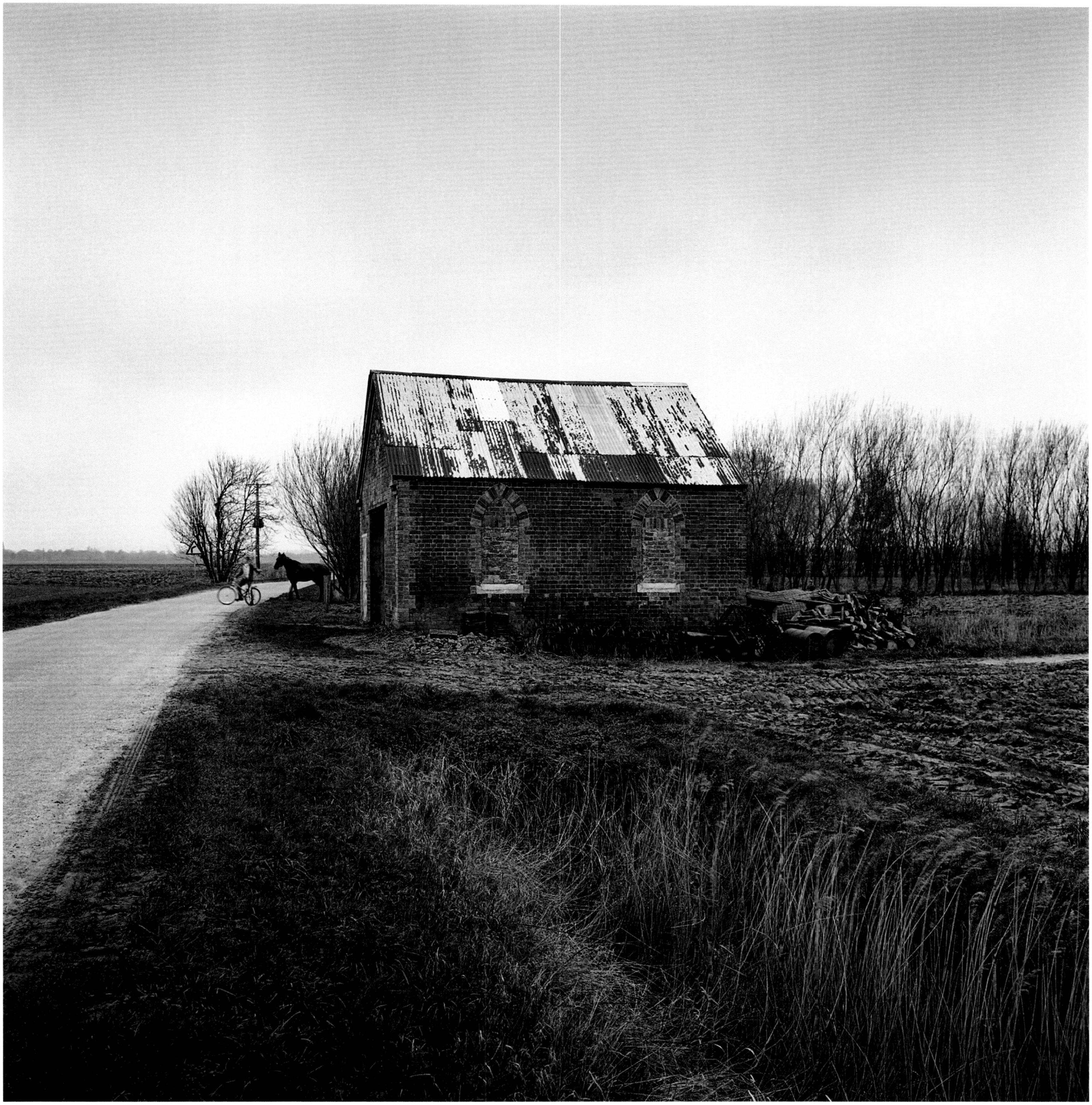

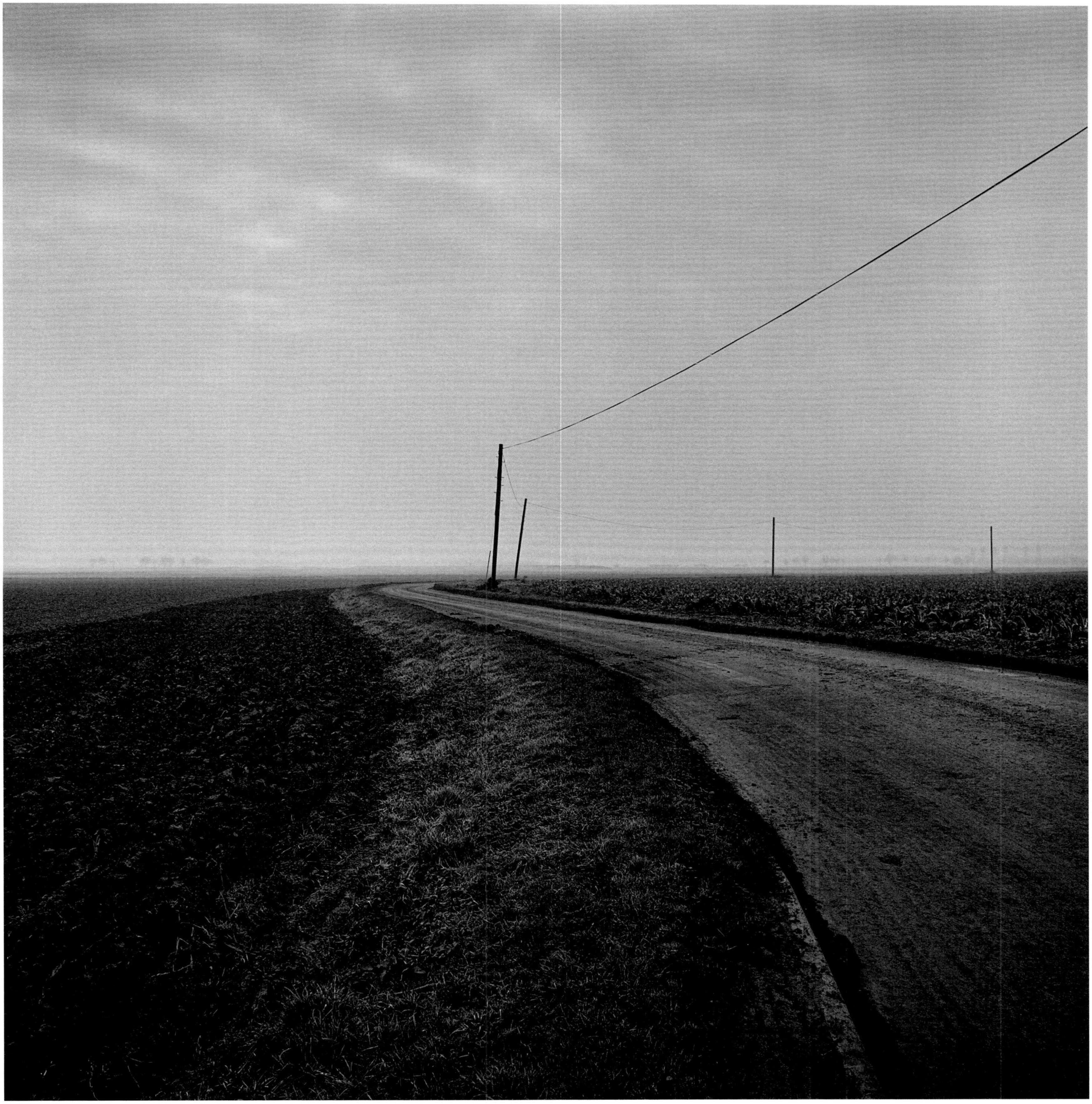

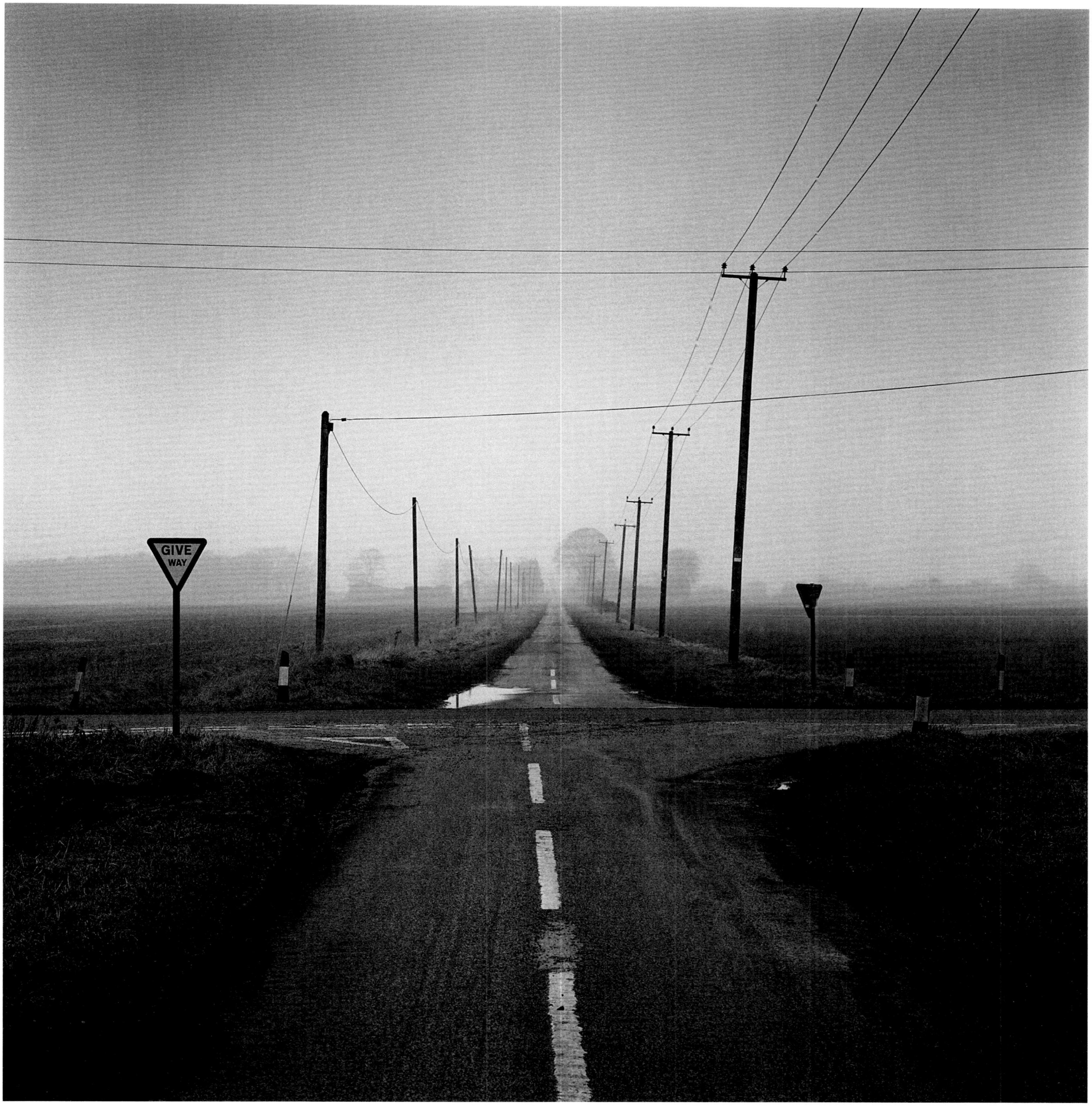
GIVE
WAY

62 | LEVERTON LUCASGATE

following pages: FRITH BANK | MEDLAM DRAIN

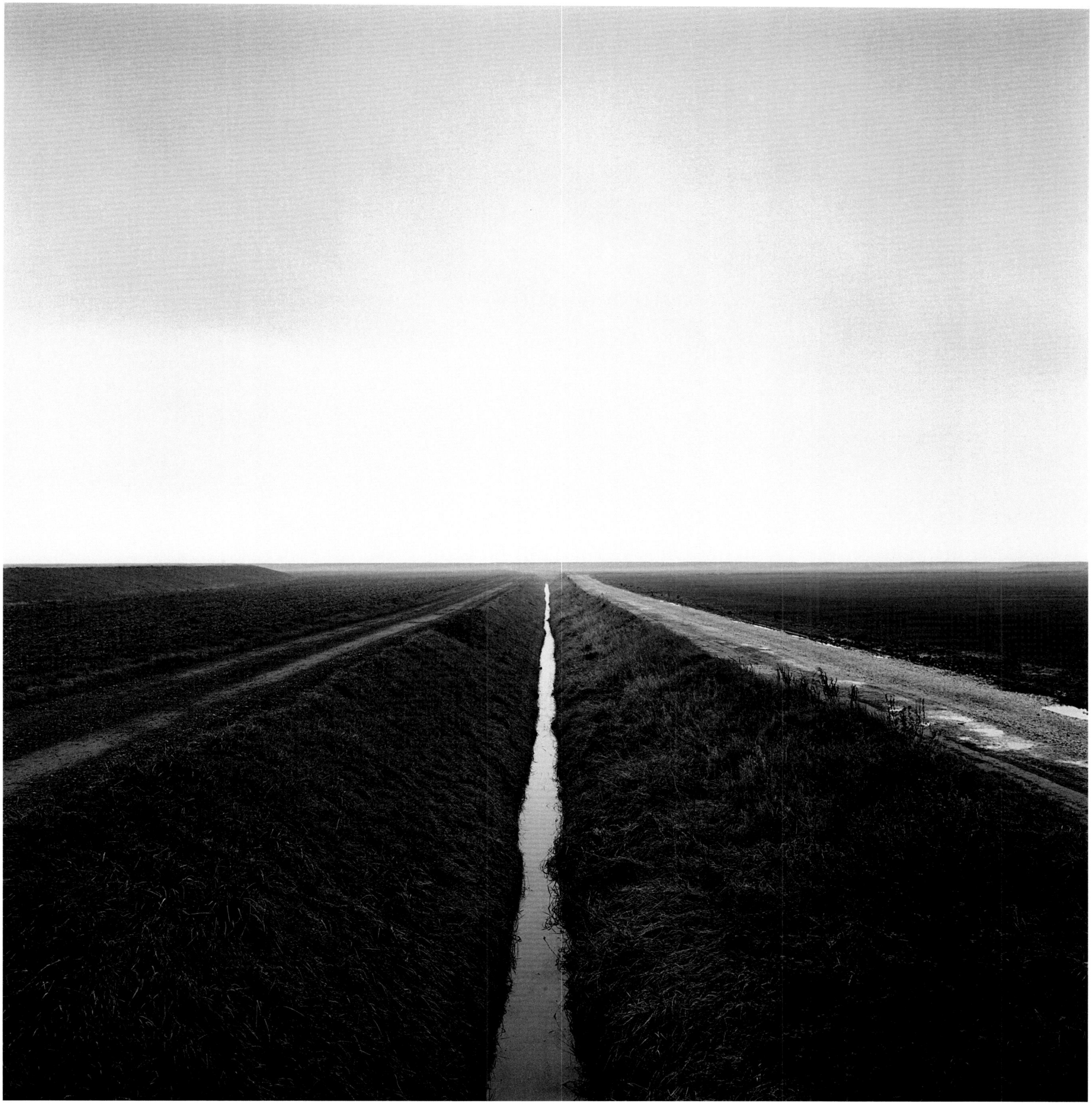

following pages: HALL FARM | NEW MARSH

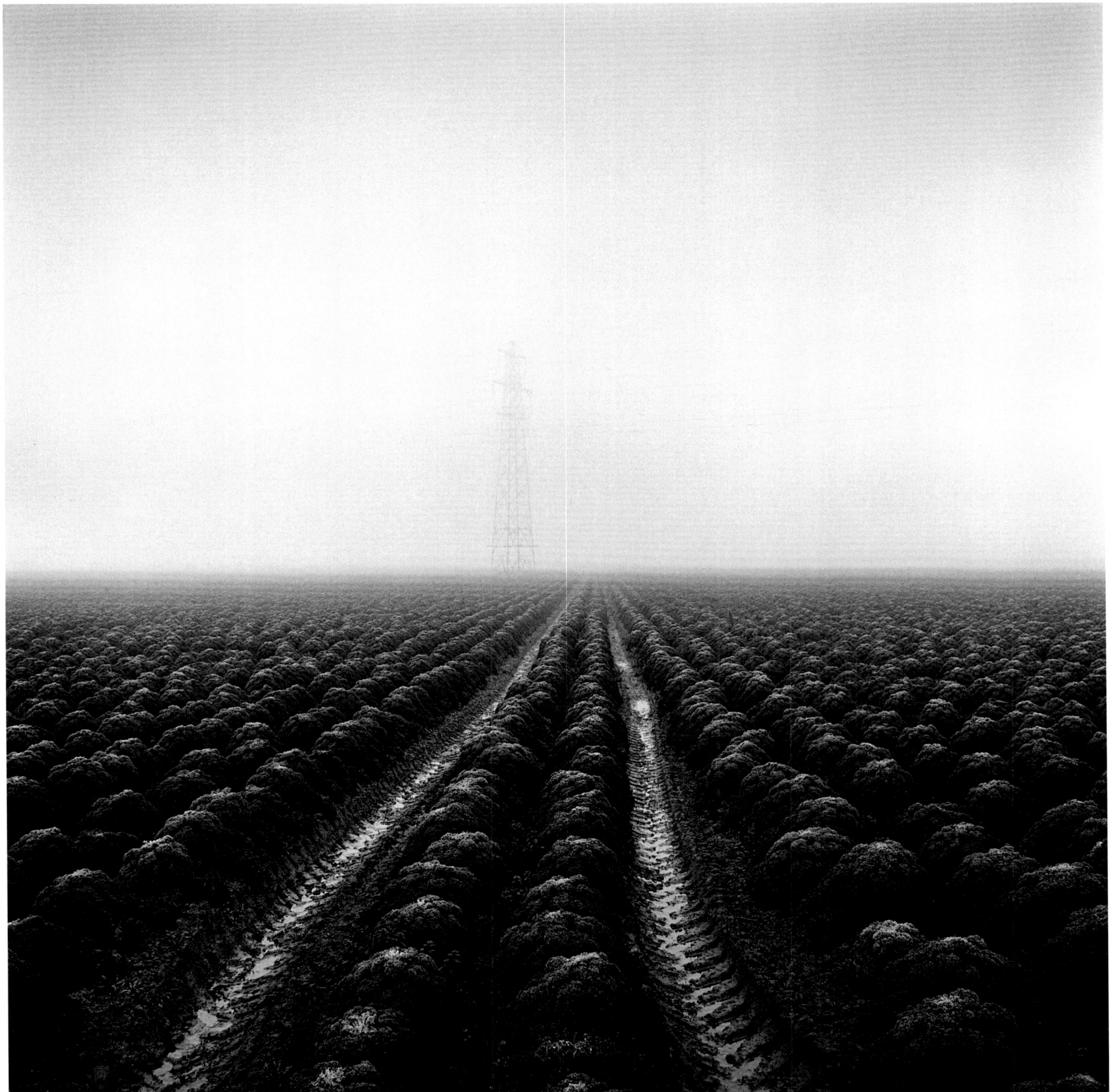

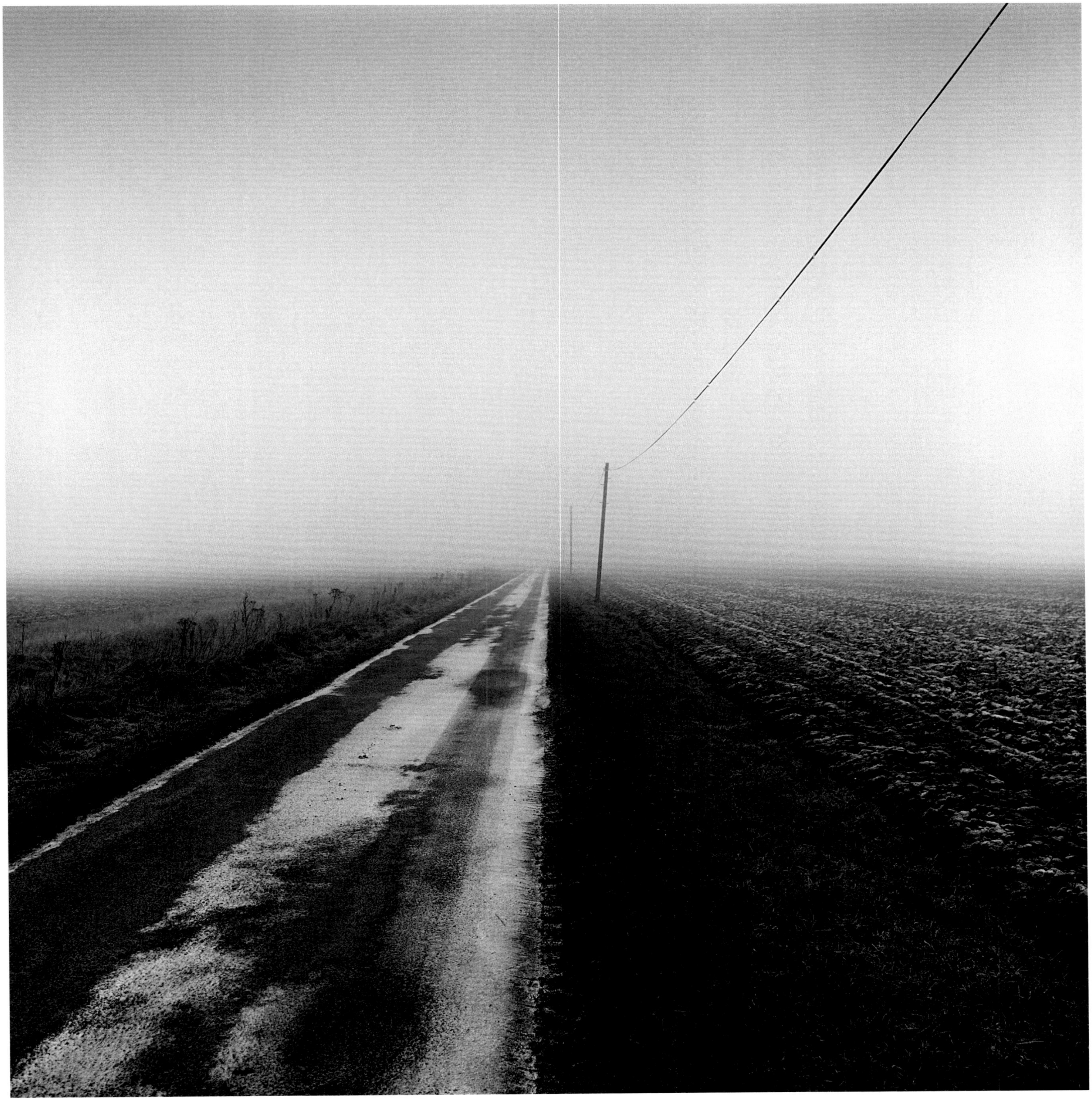

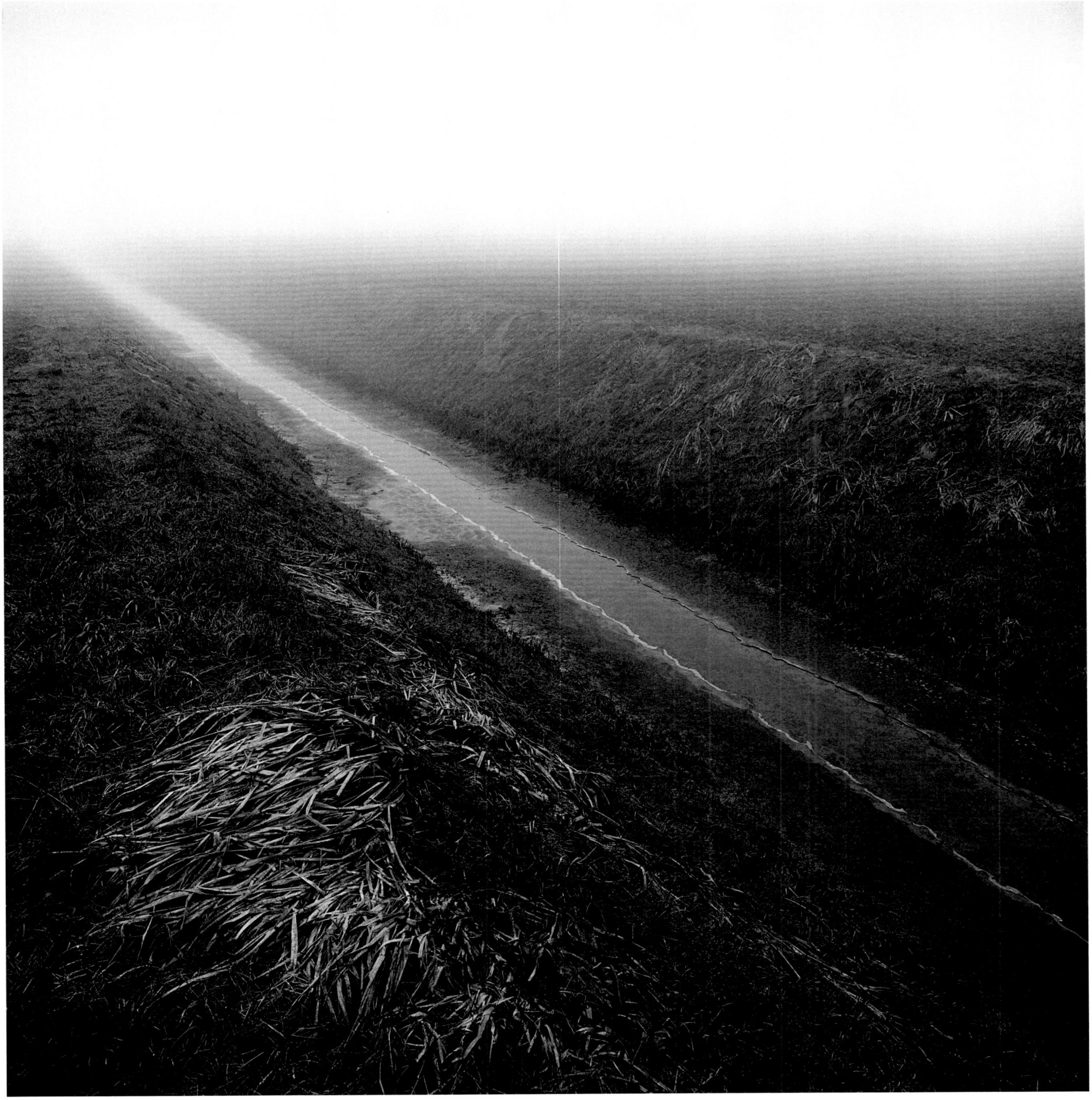

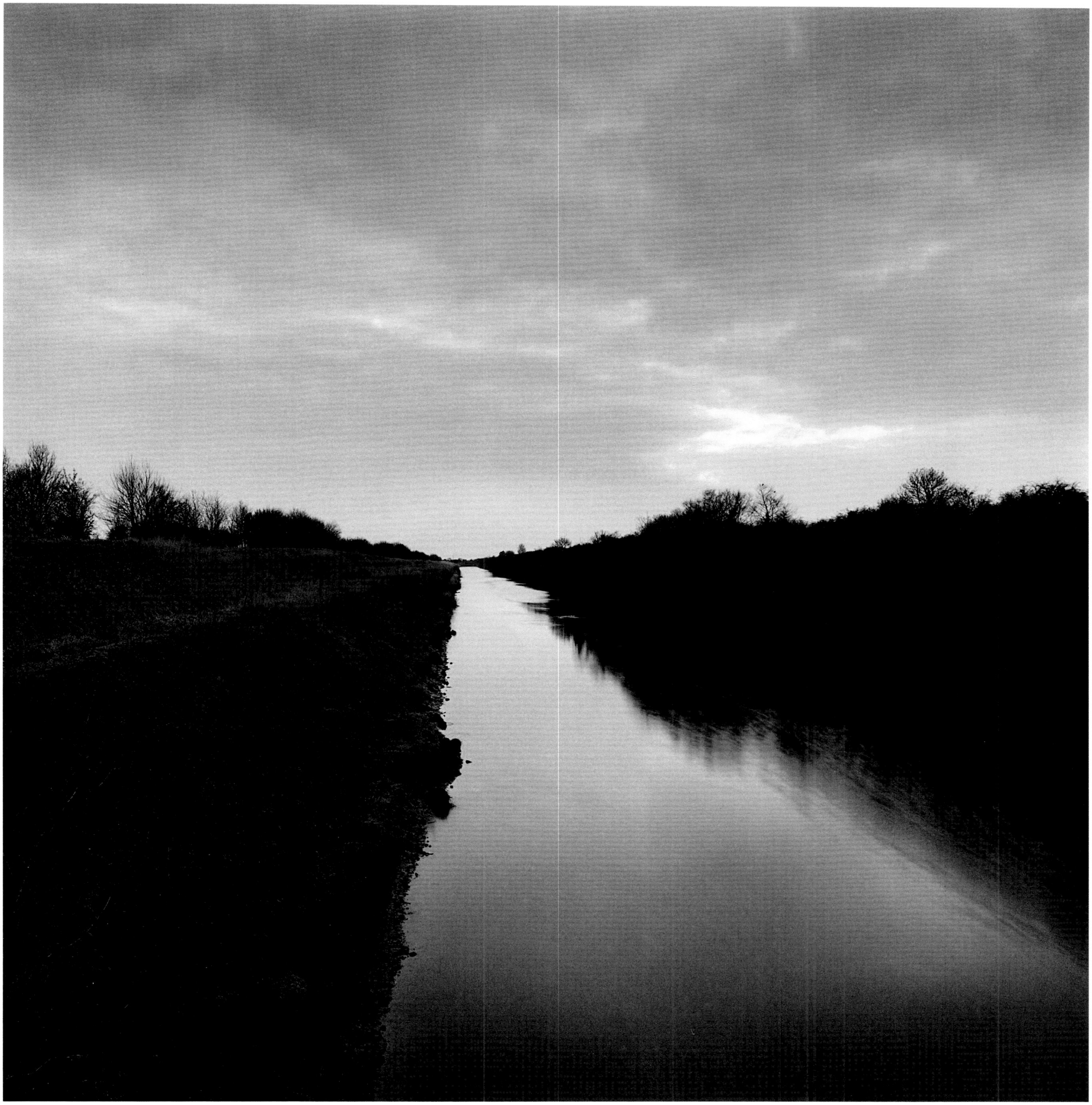

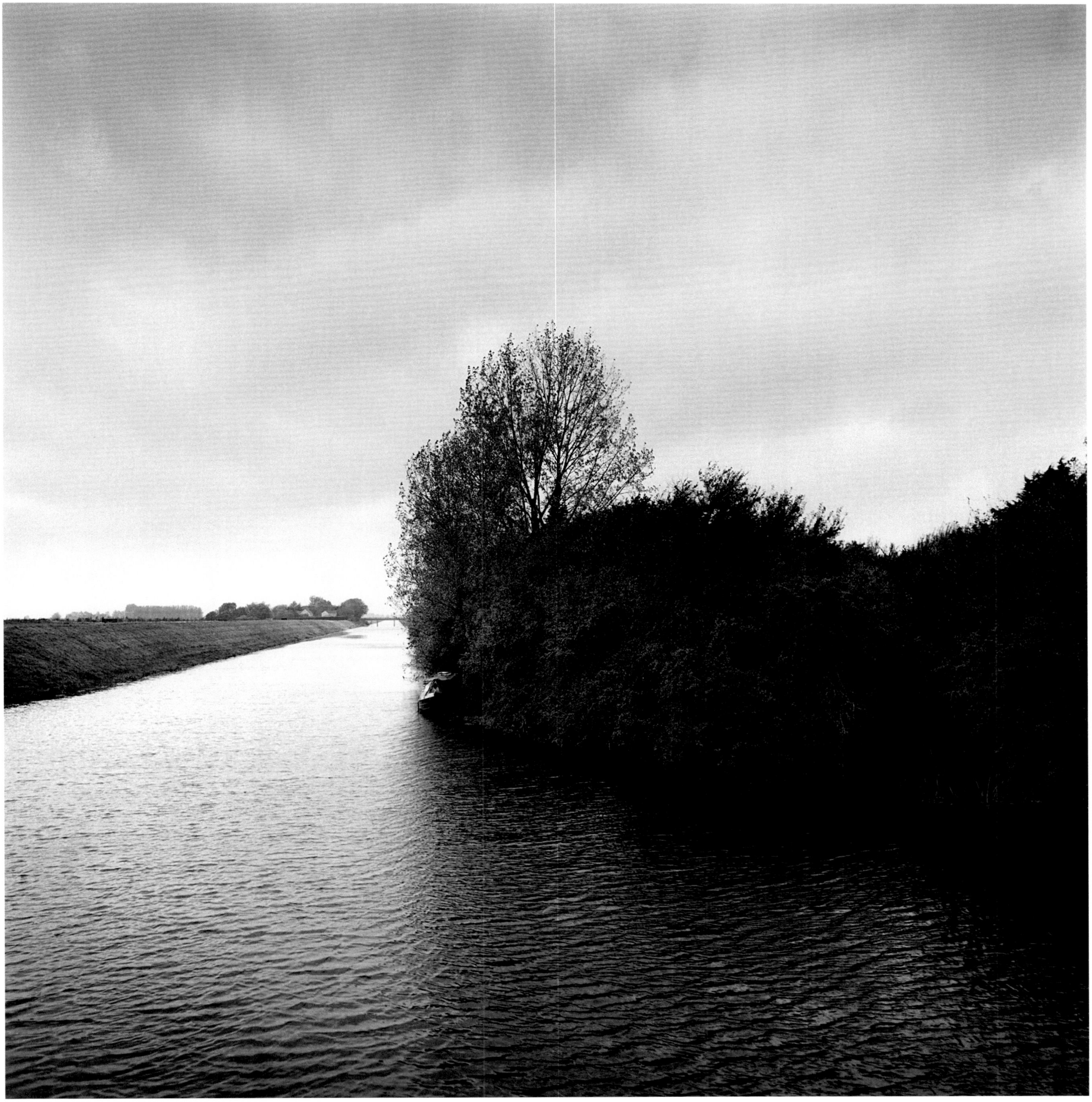

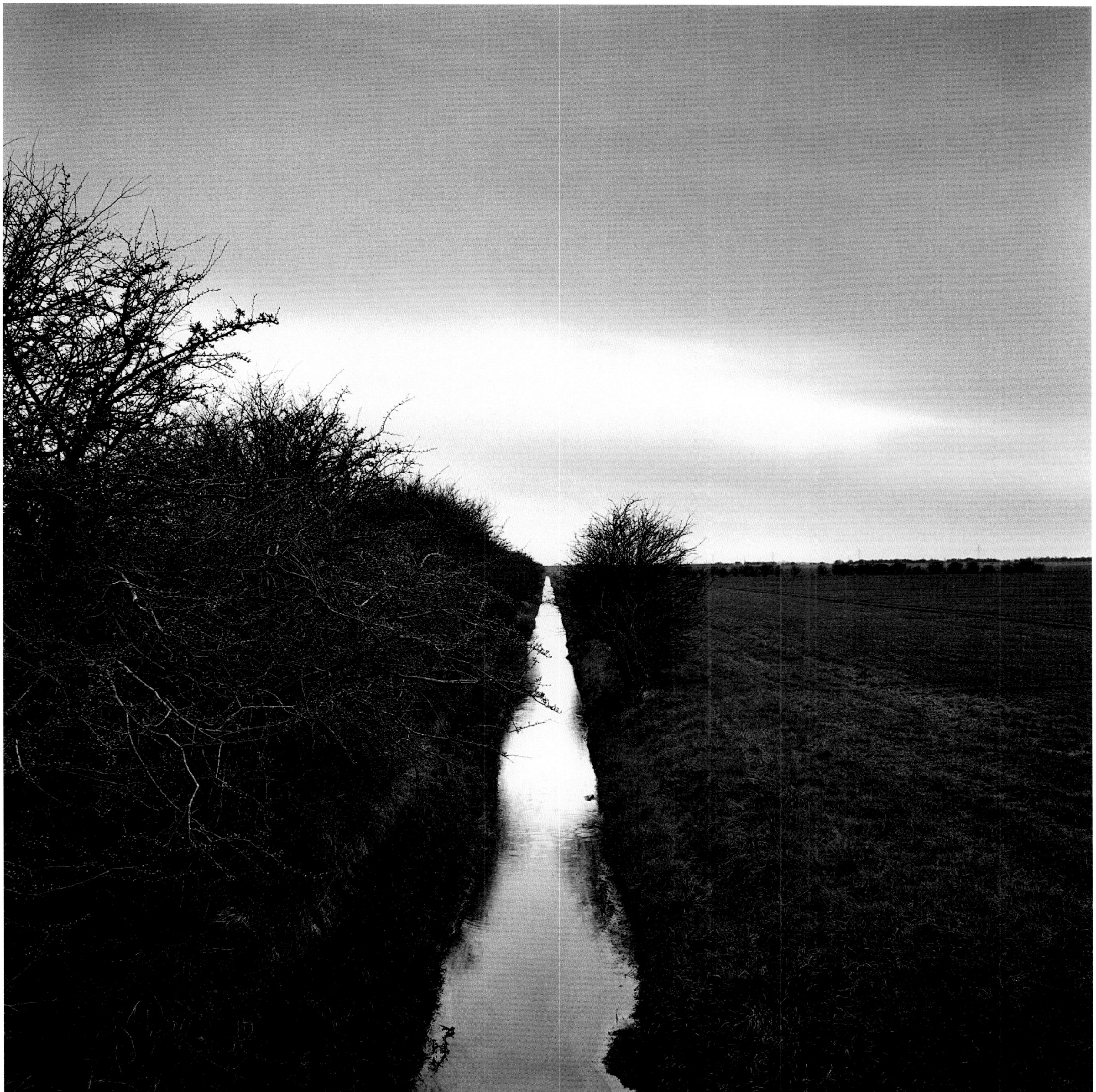

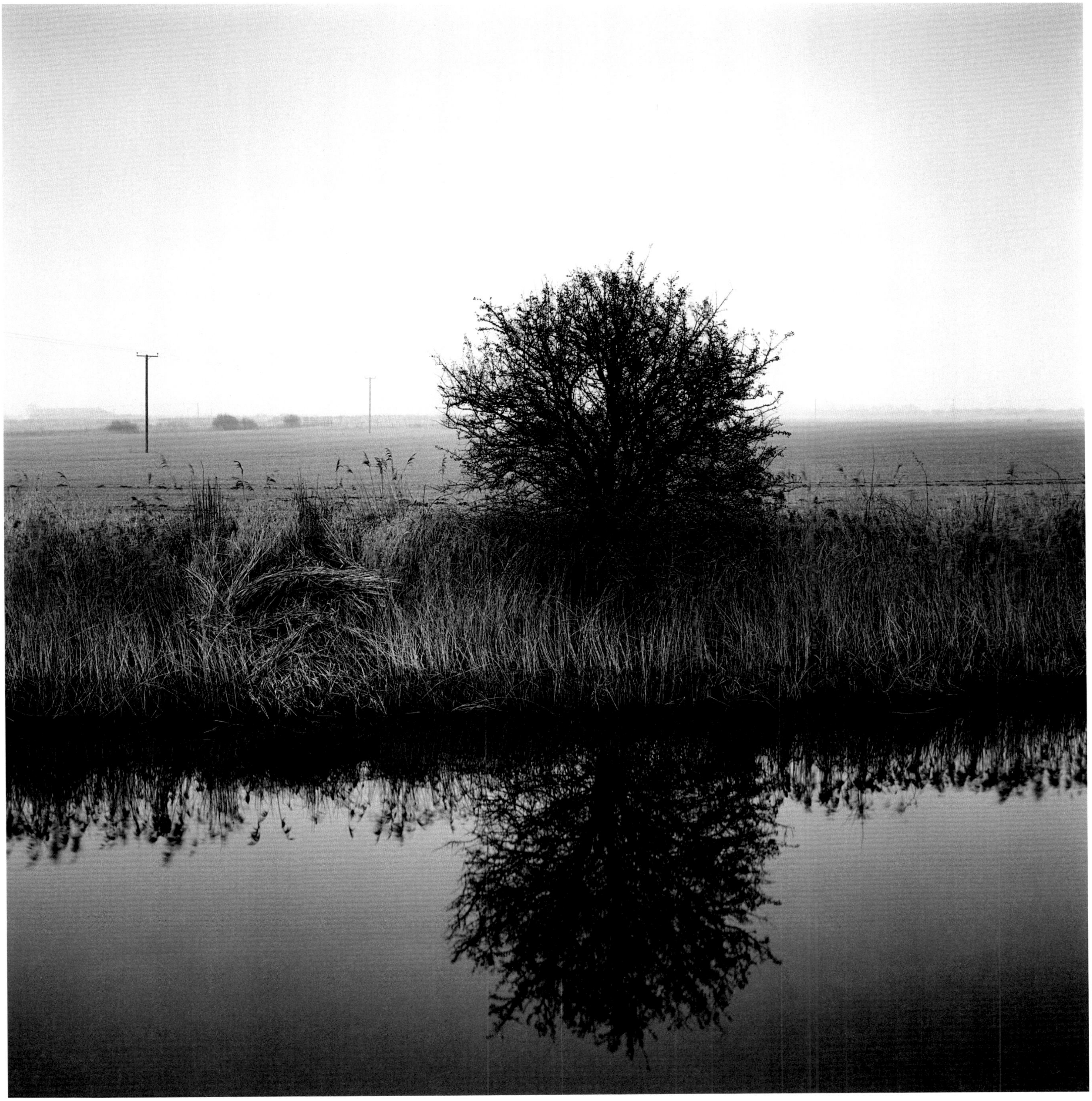

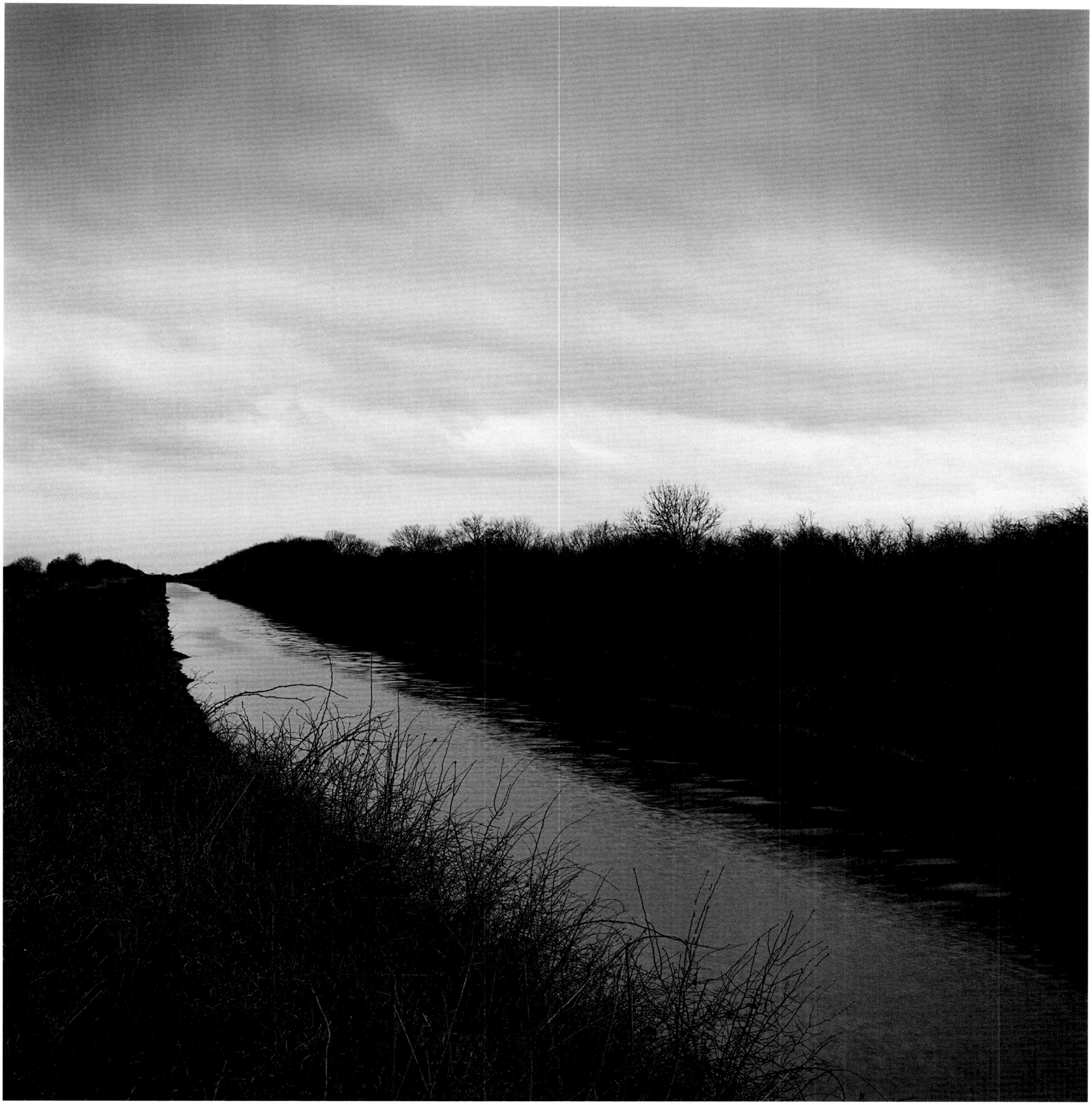

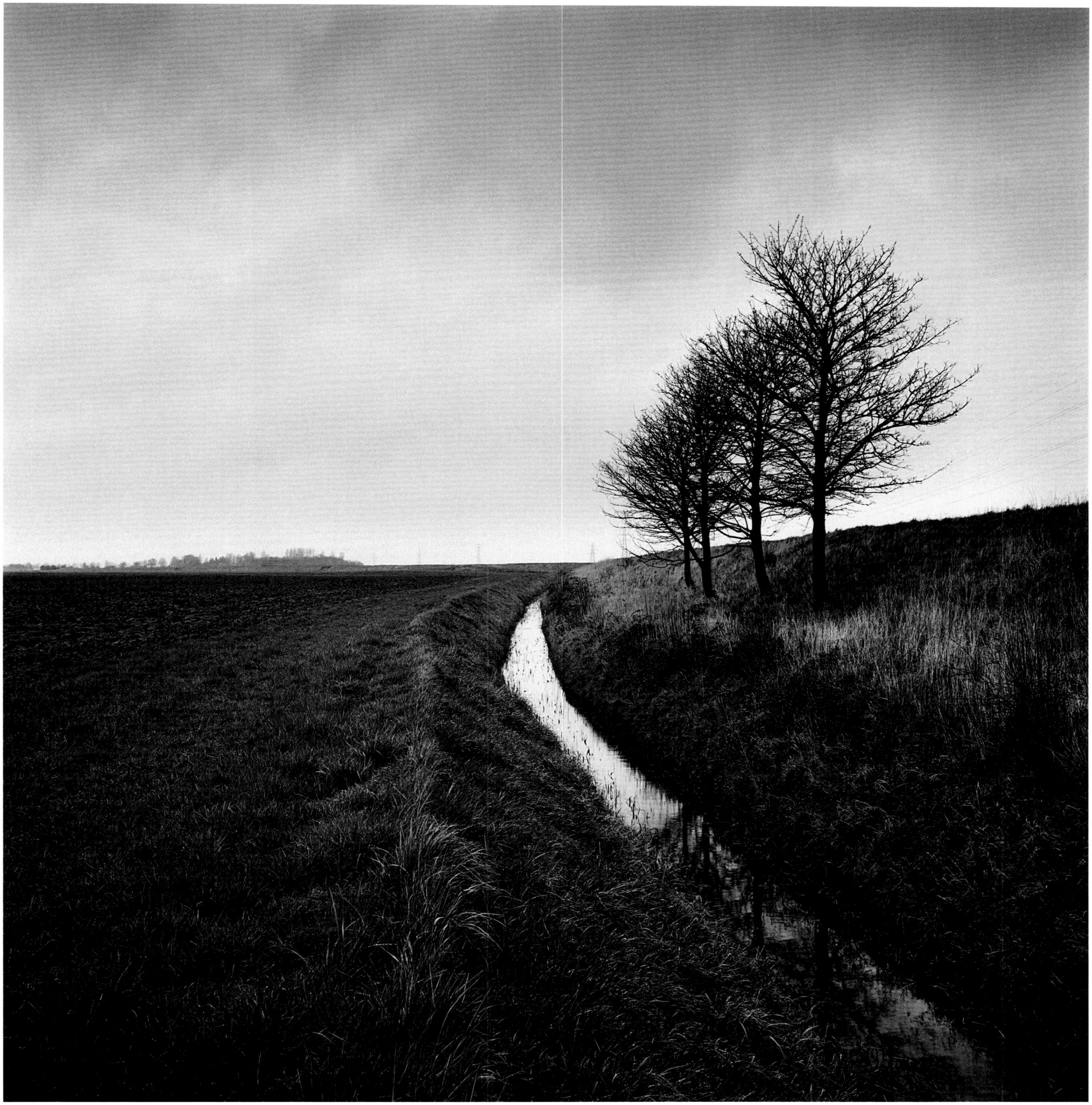

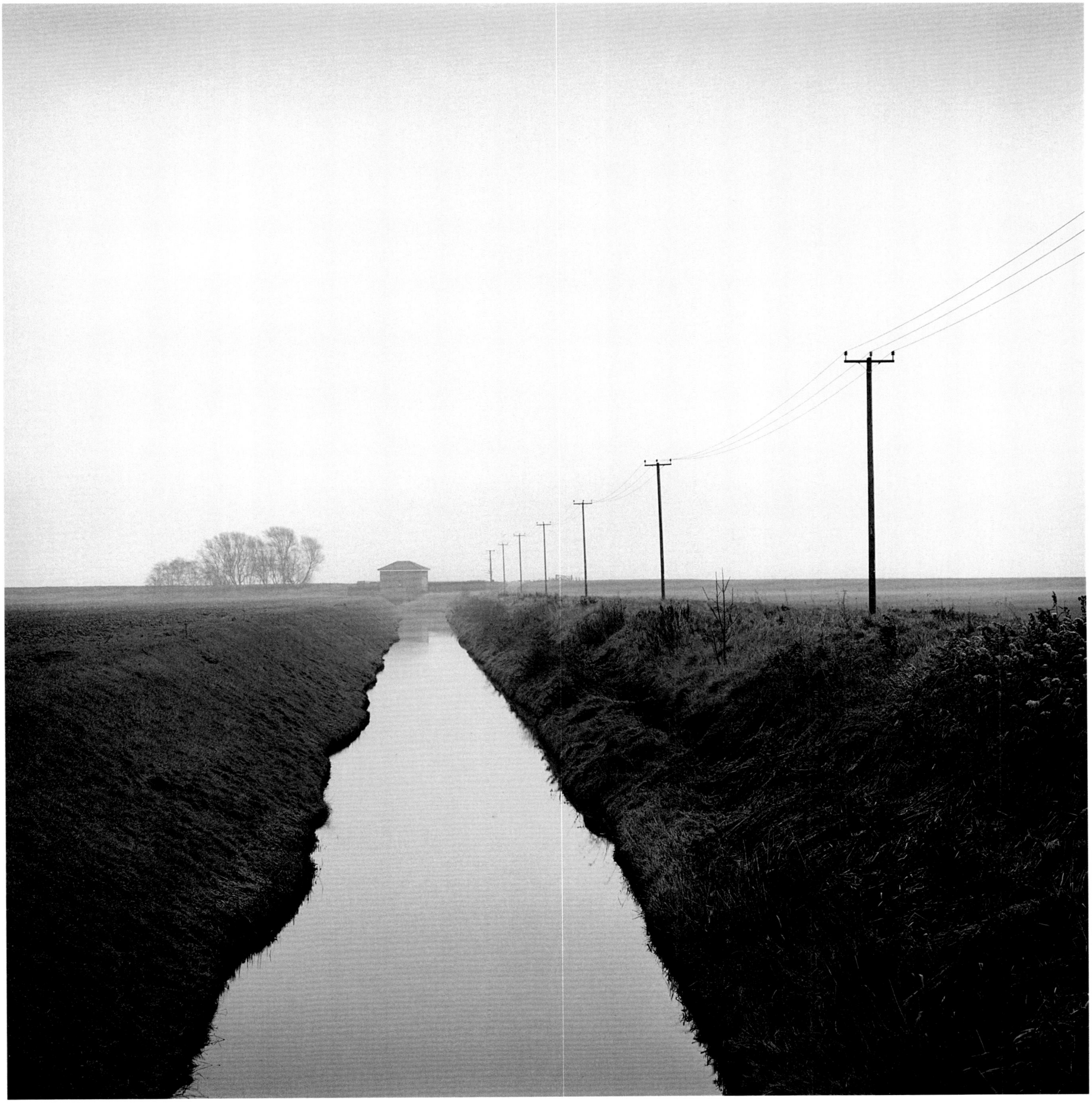

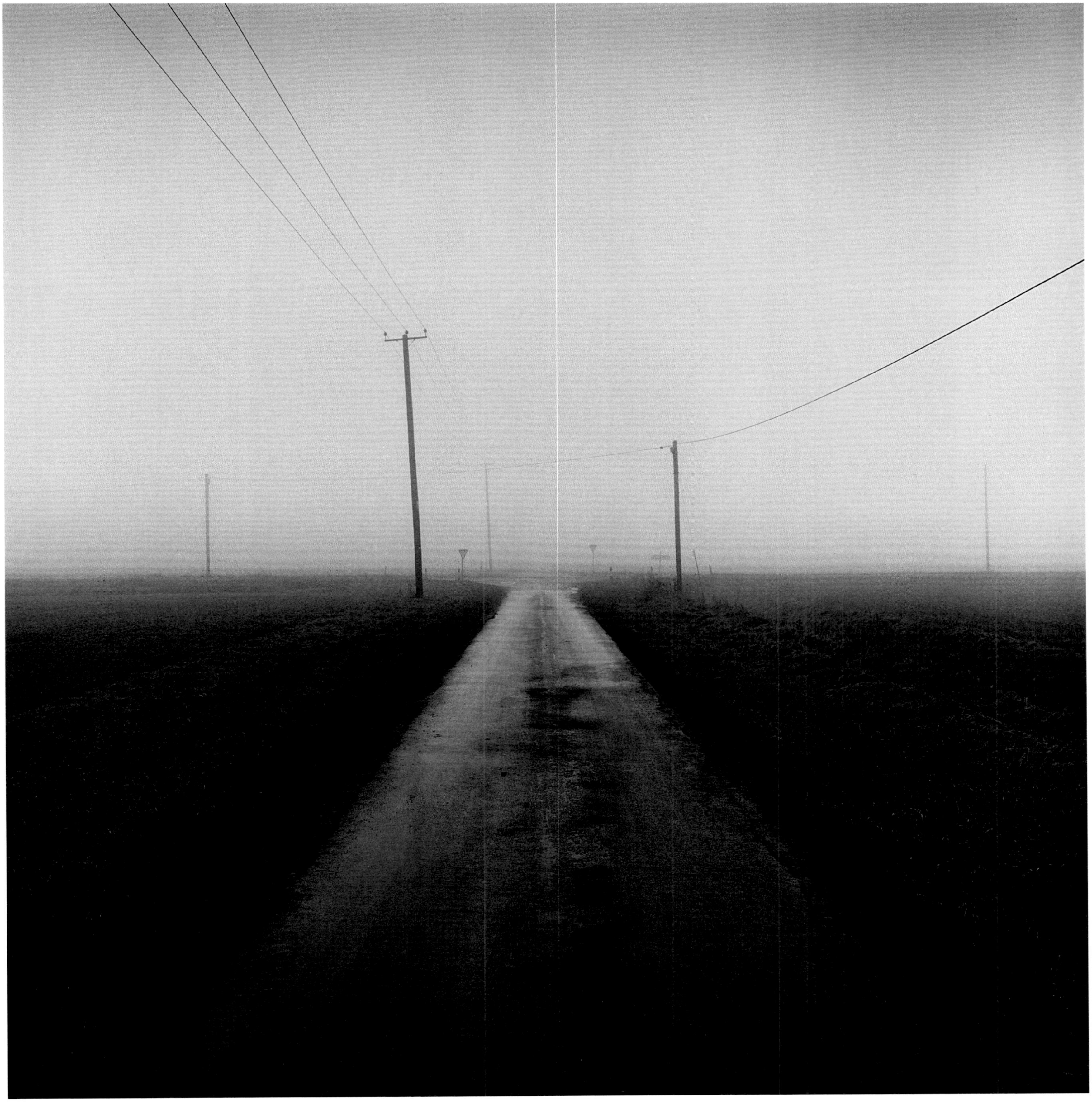

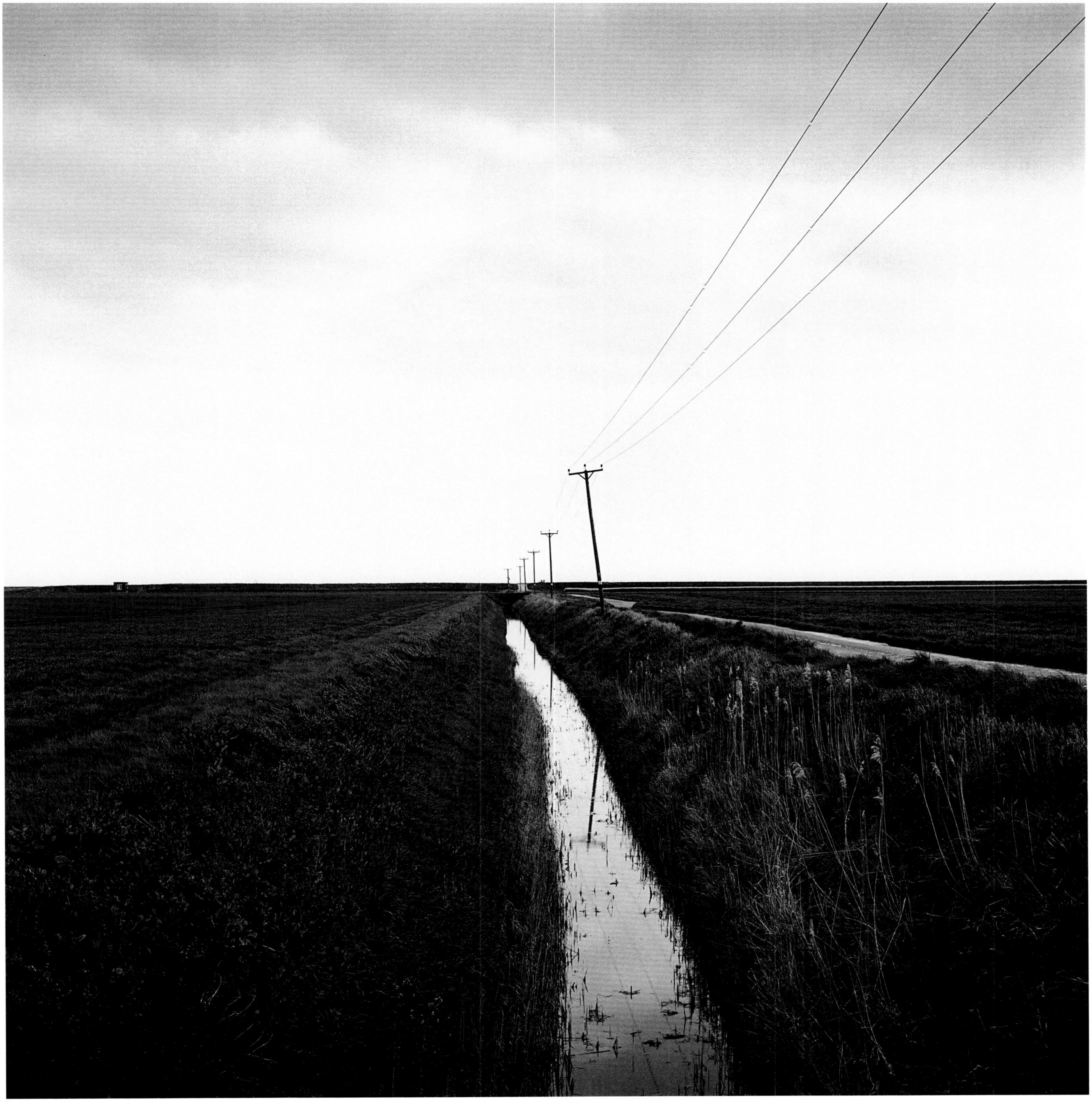

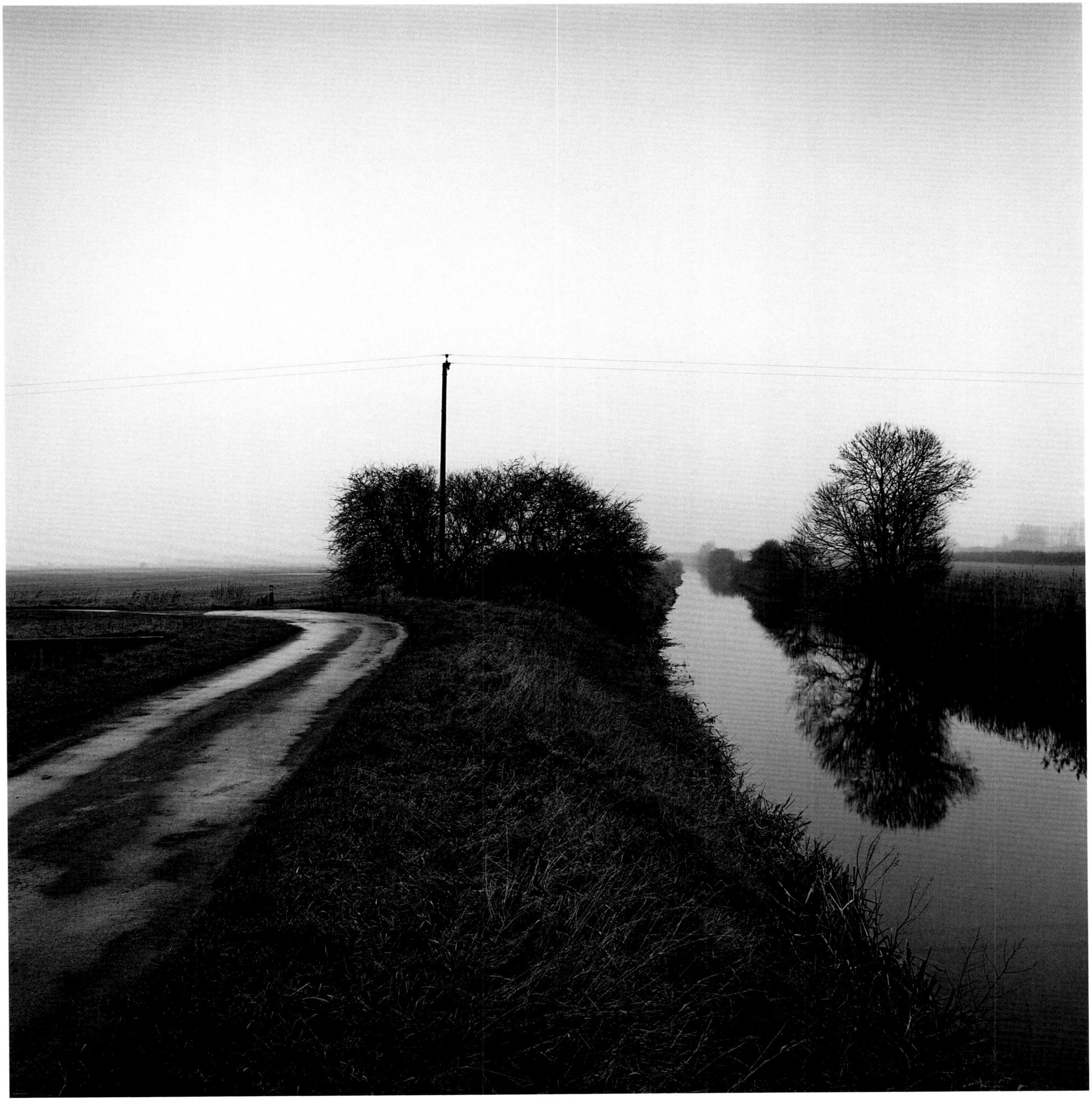

ACKNOWLEDGEMENTS

Thanks to Dewi and Caroline for all their support and encouragement through the years.

Heartfelt thanks to Francis Hodgson for his understanding of this land,
and his wonderful and insightful interpretation of these pictures.

Deepest gratitude to Ivor Braka for his passionate appreciation of my work.

And special thanks to ILFORD PHOTO for their long standing support.

Paul Hart

DRAINED is the second book in a three part series on the Fenlands in the UK.

The reproductions in this book are from direct scans of original silver gelatin prints made by Paul Hart.

First published in the UK in 2018 by
Dewi Lewis Publishing
8, Broomfield Road
Heaton Moor, Stockport SK4 4ND
www.dewilewis.com

ISBN 978-1-911306-37-5

Original book concept: Paul Hart
Artwork production: Dewi Lewis Publishing

Printed in Italy by EBS, Verona

Reprinted January 2020